I0620124

Fleeing to Freedom

A Family's Inspiring Ocean Escape from Vietnam to America

Quynh Nguyen Forss

Fleeing to Freedom: A Family's Inspiring Ocean Escape from Vietnam to America by Quynh Nguyen Forss

Published by Q Publishing Group

Copyright © 2022 Quynh Nguyen Forss

All rights reserved. No portion of this book may be reproduced in any form without permission from the publisher, except as permitted by U.S. copyright law.

ISBN: 979-8-218-00032-5 (ebook)
ISBN: 979-8-218-00031-8 (paperback)

Photos courtesy of BBC News

Dedication

This book is dedicated to my dad and mom.

Thank you, Ba and Ma, for doing the impossible.
Because of that, thank you for making everything possible.

Table of Contents

Prologue

The Vietnam War was a turbulent time in history. Vietnam was divided politically into two regions: the communist North and the democratic South. The North wanted to unify the entire nation under its communist regime. The South wanted to remain a republic and rejected the communist ideology. Fighting began in 1955.

The United States became involved in the war to help South Vietnam stop the spread of communism. By 1969, more than five hundred thousand Americans were stationed in the country.

Meanwhile, the Soviet Union poured weapons and military advisors into the North. The United States and the Soviet Union were rival superpowers during this period, competing for domination on the world stage.

On April 30, 1975, North Vietnamese soldiers stormed Saigon, the capital of South Vietnam, and raised the communist flag. The war was over. The North was victorious and the South had lost.

The communists immediately sent South Vietnamese military commanders, religious leaders, and thousands of others who supported the old government to reeducation camps. They were sent to learn about the new regime. Many endured torture and starvation while being forced to do hard labor.

As the new government began imposing its political and economic structure, people in the southern part of Vietnam started fleeing the country. They feared violence and oppression from the ruling North Vietnamese if they stayed. Hundreds of thousands escaped by boat on the South China Sea to places like Hong Kong and Singapore.

It's estimated that more than one million refugees fled from 1975 to 1995. It was common for family members to flee at separate times to help ensure that at least some would survive and find a safe haven. Desperate families crowded on small wooden boats that were not suitable for the immense and unpredictable expanse of the South China Sea. These people were willing to risk everything in search of a better life. Thousands didn't survive the voyage.

Those who fled by sea became known as the "boat people." My family is among them.

This is our story.

Boat Escape

July 1, 1979

They had to move quickly.

"Where are we going?" asked five-year-old Quynh.

She and her twenty-six-year-old mother, whose name was Nga, and her four-year-old sister, Nhu, were walking down the creaky stairs outside their house—and the sun was not yet awake.

"Not so loud, Quynh. We have to be quiet," said Ma, who paused on the last step and looked around. When she saw nothing but the surrounding trees and heard nothing but the night bugs, she ushered her girls off the stairs and toward a rumbling noise.

"Why do we have to be quiet?" whispered Quynh.

They turned a corner and saw a motorcycle idling. Leaning against it was Uncle Truong.

"Go to your uncle," said Ma. She let go of the girls and stood against the house. Sweat had built on her forehead, and she rubbed her stomach.

Uncle Truong picked up Nhu and set her at the front of the motorcycle. "Now, hold on tight," he said. He sat behind her and helped Quynh get behind him.

"Uncle Truong, where are we going?" asked Quynh, rubbing her eyes as she suppressed a yawn.

"Ma will tell you soon," Truong said. "Hold on to me tight."

Quynh wrapped her arms around her uncle and waited.

Ma moved away from the building and walked to them.

"Are you all right?" Truong asked Ma.

Ma just nodded her head and settled in behind Quynh. She then grabbed Truong's shoulders. "Go. Hurry."

Truong revved the engine, and they all took off into the night. Ma turned around and saw some of her neighbors peeking out of their windows, wondering who would be up at such an early hour. She wondered what they were thinking: Another family trying to escape? Did they have a family emergency? Was the baby ready?

Ma turned away, put a hand on her protruding belly, and prayed that the neighbors wouldn't ask questions and wouldn't turn in her family members who had to stay behind.

The streets were dark and silent. The only visitors outside the closed shops and cafés were the shadows.

The wind played with the girls' hair and seeped through their clothes and onto their skin. Quynh shivered and shook, missing the comfort of her bed and the warmth of her blanket. *Why did we have to leave?* she wondered. *Where are we going? Why do we have to be quiet?*

Truong slowed the motorcycle down as they reached the docks. Quynh peered around her uncle and saw the ocean, black as a witch's brew. There was only one white patch where the moon was reflecting off the water.

The motorcycle came to a halt, and everyone got off. At the docks was a man bathed in darkness, standing next to a boat. Quynh, seeing the dark shadow, hid behind her mother.

"What?" asked Ma.

Quynh pointed ahead, and Ma took her hand. "It will be all right." She took Nhu's hand and faced Truong. "Thank you," she said.

Truong offered her a sad smile and hugged her tight. "I pray you all make it safely." He got down on his knees and hugged his nieces with all his love. He realized how small they were and how huge the ocean was. The waters, if given the chance, would swallow them whole. "You girls look after your mother and father."

As Truong let them go, his arms trembled. He wanted to hold each one a second longer. He got on his motorcycle and took off, leaving behind little dirt clouds. He looked back and wondered whether that was the last time he would be able to hold them.

"Where is he going?" asked Nhu.

Ma turned her girls to the boat. "Come on."

As they got closer and closer to the dark man, Quynh tried to break free of her mother's grasp.

"Quynh, stop. Behave yourself."

"But he's so scary," cried Quynh.

Once they got on the dock, the moon provided better light and the girls recognized the man. "Ba!" they cried out. They let go of their mother and hugged their father's legs.

Ba, whose name was Phu, bent down and took a hand of each girl. "I need you both to go under the boat. Hurry now," he said.

"But—" Quynh began to say.

Ma had caught up and taken the girls' hands from Ba. "You heard your father. Do as he says." She released their hands and watched the girls board the boat and descend under the wooden planks.

When it was Ma's turn, Ba helped her aboard. "Are you feeling OK?"

Ma wiped the sweat from her forehead, saying, "I'll be fine. Don't worry about me."

"The girls," Ba said. "Did you ..."

Ma gave a firm nod. "I did."

Ba let go of her and watched her disappear under the planks. She lay between Quynh and Nhu and sighed deeply. Ma folded her hands on top of her balloon-sized belly, ready to pop at any moment. Nine months pregnant, she was due in exactly a week.

Ba thought there was no better time to leave than while she was pregnant; others wouldn't expect that a family would attempt to escape with a pregnant wife. People wouldn't believe that they would flee and, in the process, risk the lives of the mother and her unborn child.

Ma hummed softly, rubbing her belly and wondering if her family would be blessed with another baby girl or their first boy.

Waiting at the docks in Da Nang, a central coastal city, Ba watched as more and more people in small groups came to the boat and went under to join his family. Each group came every five minutes so that they wouldn't rouse suspicion. One group included Ba's younger sister and younger brother, Tam and Du.

Below the planks, Quynh's and Nhu's eyes got heavy. The waves rocking the boat and the stillness of the night put them to sleep. Ma sighed in relief and licked her lips. Before they left, she had slipped sleeping pills in the girls' food. She wanted them quiet and asleep so they could get past the guards.

Once everyone was aboard, Ba's childhood friend, Son, began to cover the boat with blankets. Ba helped him cover the people below. Son then grabbed some fishing nets and spread them out. Ba set the fishing poles in sight for the guards to see and handed Son a *nón lá*, a rice hat in the shape of a circular cone. Son took it and, with shaking hands, put it on his head. "Ready when you are." He walked to the front of the boat and tightly gripped his fishing pole. He swallowed nervously, his mouth suddenly dry.

Ba untied their boat from the dock and pushed them to the ocean. He started the engine and—with steady, sweaty palms—steered the boat toward the South China Sea.

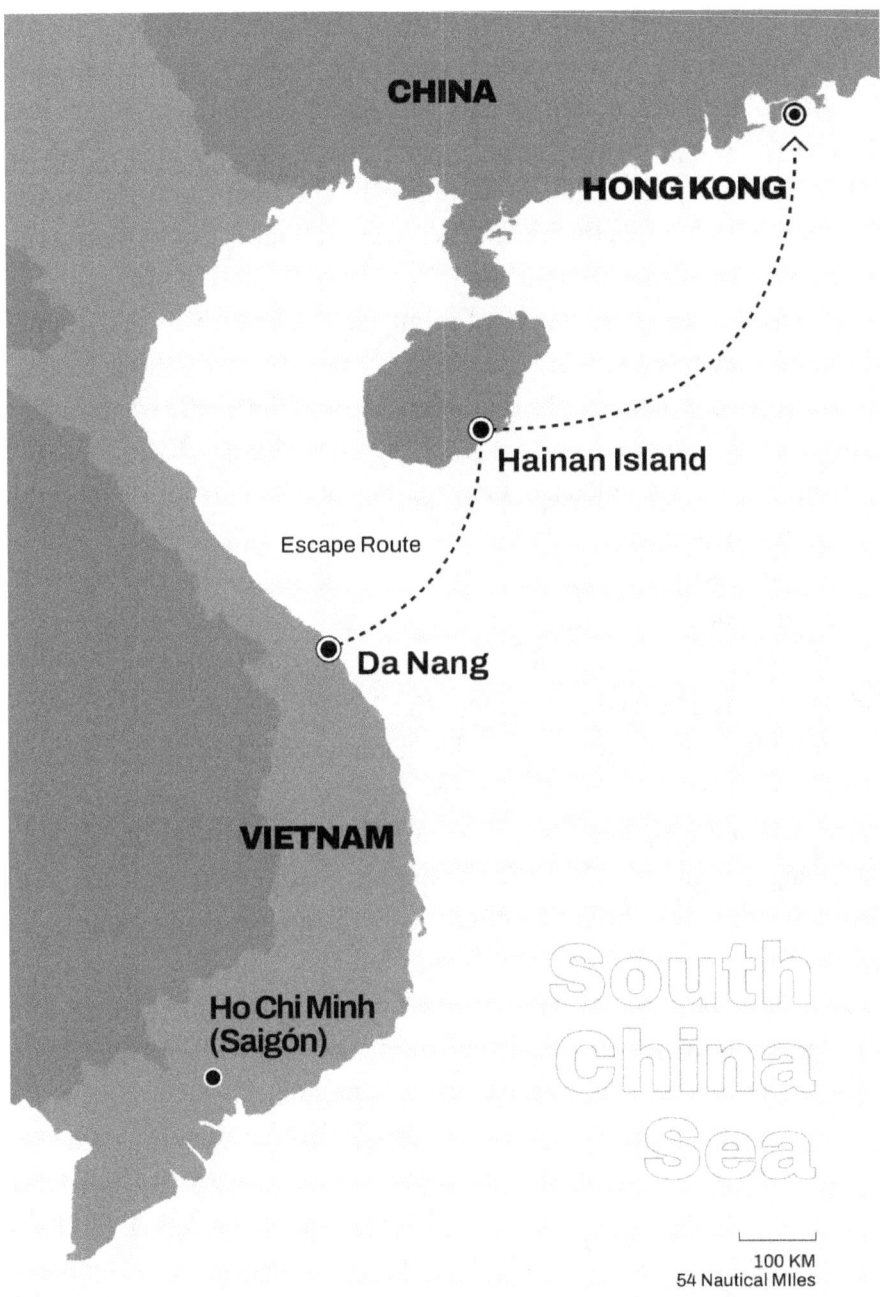

Around them, other men were at their boats, readying their nets for their morning catch. Captains ordered their crews to get the boats ready. The boats always left at sunrise and headed out to the bays or all the way out into the ocean. Seasoned fishermen hoped to get the best catches, such as prawn, squid, and fish. They checked their nets, looked over their fishing gear, and got on the boats. They started their engines or used their oars to push themselves out in the water.

All was well the first couple of minutes. The water was still, and the fishermen they passed didn't glance their way. The only thing Ba could hear was the roar of the boat's rebuilt engine and the gentle water lapping at the hull.

Something loud splashed nearby, causing Son to jump. The boat rocked and caused ripples.

"Son, it was only a fish," said Ba.

Son chuckled nervously. "Sorry."

"We can do this, Son. Think good thoughts. We're going to make it," said Ba. "We've planned this for months."

Son quickly nodded and held his fishing pole close to his body. Ba looked ahead, seeing that they were approaching the guard patrol. A guard was leaning against a shack where another guard was sitting up but fast asleep, his green army hat covering his eyes to help him sleep. Atop the small shack were bright spotlights that the guards could maneuver at their will.

This is it, Ba thought. He faced forward, straightening his posture. Ahead were more armed guards patrolling the region. Ba's eyes couldn't help but glance at the guns they held at their sides.

The boat had to get past the shore patrol without raising suspicion.

The stakes were high. Ba shuddered as he thought of what would happen if the guards stopped their boat and inspected it. Would they find all fifteen people hiding below? Would they separate the men from the women and children, and take them to jail? What would happen to his daughters? What would happen to his expectant wife? Or would the guards look at Son and Ba and kill them on the spot?

As Ba's boat drew nearer to the guards, he made his eyes focus on what lay ahead. Beyond the endless miles of ocean spread out before him, Ba saw endless miles of opportunities for his family: a new beginning, a new home. He tried to keep his thoughts on what could be and tried to ignore the guards. The boat was steady, going through the water as smoothly as a knife through butter.

Son, at the front of the boat, was moving his lips, praying—praying that they would go unnoticed, praying that they would get past the guard patrol and continue into deeper waters. The sweat gathering on his forehead slithered down his temples and dripped from his face.

Ba's heart pounded. He heard it over the boat's engine and, for a split second, thought the patrol heard it too, as a guard pinned his eyes on their boat.

The guard wore a dark-green uniform with a brown belt buckled around his waist. It was silver and shiny, recently polished. He also wore a green cap with a bright-red star in the middle, indicating he worked for the communist government. In his hands was a gun, ready to be used.

Ba and Son tried not to flinch at the sight of it. From his days on the battlefield, Ba knew too well of the damage that a gun could cause.

The guard looked right through Ba and carried on. He didn't care about a little fishing boat. Even if these two fishermen were trying to escape, they wouldn't make it very far in a watercraft that small. The guard chuckled to himself, thinking back on the boats he had previously seen pass—some having turned back intact and others returning as just pieces. The guard expected to eventually see either this boat returning or wooden planks bobbing on the surface.

Ba slowed his breathing, inhaling the ocean breeze and letting it out smoothly.

Once they cruised past the guard patrol, Ba sighed in relief at the same time as Son. Ba wiped the sweat from his eyebrows and grinned. Son smiled at him, and his grip loosened on the fishing pole.

"We did it," gasped Son, a nervous laugh escaping his lips.

"Not quite," said Ba to himself.

His hands were no longer sweaty. He kept them steady, steering the boat deeper into the ocean. And he kept his eyes forward—not once looking back. Communism had infected his country. Vietnam was no longer his home, nor was it the home of the others on the boat. For all of those on the vessel, Vietnam had become a place to fear. It was a prison. Their home was long gone when the war ended and communism took control of the land.

Ba was aware that this was just the beginning of their journey. Ahead, there were other obstacles that they had to conquer one day at a time: thieving pirates, unpredictable weather, the danger of running out of all necessary supplies to keep them alive, and the uncertainty of whether their escape plan could work at all.

Despite all the fears and risks, Ba knew the payoff would be worth it. They needed to reach Hong Kong—about six hundred miles away—and then reach their final destination. A place they would call home. A place for Ba and his family to be given a chance to rebuild their lives and have his children's dreams come true: America.

Ba looked across the blankets where his children slept, along with his life partner and their unborn child.

For them, he thought.

Now, looking over the deep-blue ocean that the sun was highlighting, Ba grasped a compass in his hand and felt hope.

First Day on Boat

July 1, 1979

The South China Sea, an endless glass of deep blue, reflected the sun. A symbol of a new day and rebirth.

Inhaling the salty ocean tang, Quynh woke up from below and lifted off the blanket covering the wooden planks. She looked out as far as she could over the ocean blue. It seemed to never end, this endless display of water. The wind gently moved her hair back from her face.

Quynh peered below at her mother and asked, "Now can you tell me where we're going?"

With a soft smile and a protective hand over her protruding belly, Ma answered, "We're going to where my parents live, your *Bà ngoại* and ông *ngoại*. They live in a faraway place called America."

Quynh peered over the fishing boat, seagulls saying good morning and flying toward the sun.

America, Quynh thought dreamily.

A place she heard others speak of so fondly. A country full of freedom and liberty. A country where anything was possible as long as you had dedication and worked hard. A land that her father had said was an extraordinary place that would give them a chance to rebuild their lives. Where dreams came true.

To Quynh, America sounded like a magical place, and she couldn't wait to get there. She wondered what sights she would witness and what she would be able to experience for the first time.

As Quynh and the other sixteen people on the boat made their voyage across the sea, she didn't understand the wounded looks being cast back toward Vietnam. There was pain in their eyes as they left behind the country where they had always lived, created memories, and experienced their biggest moments.

Ma came from below and sat on a wooden plank. Quynh crawled over to her. "Ma?"

"Hmm?"

"What about *Bà Nội* and *Ông Nội* back in Vietnam?" Quynh said, referring to her paternal grandparents. "Are they coming with us to America?"

Ma shook her head and put an arm around Quynh. "Not now."

"Will I ever see them again?"

Ma looked back at her home country. "I hope one day."

Ma and Ba looked back, their home country getting smaller as the boat sailed on. Vietnam was where they were born, grew up, got married, and created a family. Memories brought tears to Ma's eyes. She looked down at her ring.

Ba and Ma met in 1970, nearly ten years earlier, at a friend's birthday party. Both had just turned seventeen.

Ma helped bring a cake outside and set it on a table. She moved it to the center of the table and began sticking candles into the white frosting. Van, Ma's childhood best friend, came out of her house carrying plates, napkins, and silverware. She set them next to the cake and hugged Ma. "Thank you so much for your help today."

Ma smiled at her. "Of course."

They set up the rest of the party, getting tables and chairs ready. It was a warm day and the weather was perfect. The sun wasn't too blistering, and there was no wind to move stuff about.

As Ma and Van were finishing up, a few guests streamed in.

"Can you set up the stereo while I greet them?" asked Van.

"Yeah, no problem. Go on," said Ma.

Ma plugged in the stereo and shuffled through the tapes, trying to decide what music to play first.

"I'd pick that one," said a voice behind her.

Ma jumped, the tapes falling to the ground. Her eyes widened and her heart fluttered. Before her was a young man around her age. He had thick, full, black hair and gentle brown eyes that were looking at her curiously.

"Sorry," he said, giving her a soft smile. "Didn't mean to startle you."

Both bent down to pick up the tapes. Ma chuckled nervously, feeling her cheeks turn pink. "I'm sorry. I wasn't paying attention."

Both stood up and Ba held out a tape. "This one. I'd recommend this one to play."

As Ma took it, their fingers brushed against each other. She gave him a smile. "Why this one? Are you a music expert?"

Ma set the other tapes to the side and put the tape in the stereo.

"You could say that," he said. "I'm in a band."

Ma pressed Play on the stereo and raised her eyebrows. "A band? That's impressive."

Ba looked at her as if trying to memorize her features. Her brown hair was short and framed her jaw. Highlighted by the sun, her brown eyes turned caramel.

"I'm Phu," he said.

"Hi, nice to meet you. I'm Nga," she replied, tucking strands of hair behind her ear.

They began dating after the birthday party. They were married in November 1972 and had their first child, Quynh, the following July.

Ba & Ma in Vietnam, 1973. Photo courtesy of Nguyen Family.

Even though she knew she was looking back at Vietnam, Ma didn't recognize it. The country she once called home had forced her parents and now Ba and her to leave behind his family and all their possessions.

Ba put his hand on Ma's shoulder and gave her a gentle squeeze. "We'll cherish the memories," he said.

She smiled and squeezed back.

For months, all they had been able to think about was their escape, and they hardly had any time to reflect on what it all meant. And yet, as they looked forward to Hong Kong, there was something sparkling in their eyes that they hadn't felt in a long time: hope. No one knew what their future might hold, but everyone on that boat agreed that it was better than staying in Vietnam and living under communism.

Ba lit a cigarette, and Quynh plopped down next to Ma. "I'm hungry."

Ma grabbed a nearby bag and put a handful of rice in Quynh's hands. "Eat up. Here, Nhu." She put some rice in Nhu's hands and helped her eat every single grain.

The others on the boat each had a small portion of rice. They had enough food to last only three days, which was how long Ba thought it would take to reach a refugee camp in Hong Kong.

Packed in the other bags were instant rice and noodles, five gallons of water, rice wine, and cigarettes. Next to the food and water supplies was another bag, which was packed with items just in case Ma went into labor: a small knife, a pair of nursing scissors, a spool of thread, towels, a baby blanket, two cans of condensed milk, cloth diapers, a baby bottle, and baby clothing.

No one had been allowed to bring extra clothes, personal belongings, or even suitcases because there wasn't a lot of room on the small boat. They didn't want to draw attention when they passed the shore patrol.

Ba took a drag from his cigarette, moved his head back, and let out a swirl of smoke. He steered the boat northeast, toward their destination, about six hundred miles away. Waiting for them there was a refugee camp.

It was Sunday. Ba was thinking they would get there by Wednesday. He had heard this time estimate from previous refugees.

With his compass in hand, he held it forty-five degrees northeast, the direction toward Hong Kong. Looking out over the deep-blue water, Ba saw no landmarks, so he had to rely heavily on his compass. Their boat was the only visible thing.

With a cigarette hanging from his chapped lips, Ba scanned the horizon. The ocean was full of other risks that they had to get past. Now, having sneaked by the shore patrol, they faced the possibility of more dangers in the water. Ruthless pirates could be lurking in the sea—pirates who attacked and captured boats, pirates who robbed, raped the women, and took them as slaves and prostitutes. If Ba and the other men on the boat were to fight, they could lose their lives or be tossed overboard.

Pirates weren't the only thing in the back of Ba's mind. He looked up, where the blue sky and fluffy white clouds were a good sign. He hoped the sea would not storm up. Their boat was too small to fight against high waves and was not built to endure stormy conditions. Not only could their boat be destroyed but they could drown.

Ba looked at his small children as they lapped up every grain of rice they could eat at the moment. Water was being passed around, everyone taking only one sip. Ba took the cigarette from his mouth and flicked the ashes into the water.

When it was his turn to take a sip of water, he passed and said he'd take a drink the next time around. He hoped to save as much as he could, and he didn't eat, either. He puffed on the cigarette to keep his hunger at bay.

In addition to pirates and the weather, the boat's supply of food, water, and fuel also concerned Ba. What if the supply ran out before they reached Hong Kong? What if it took a day or two longer to get there? No one on the boat knew how to fish. And not everyone knew how to swim.

The boat engine sputtered, bringing Ba back to the present. He petted it gently, and it continued on. Ba sighed in relief. This engine had already given him and Son enough trouble in the past.

Ba and Son had both used what they had in their savings—a combined ten ounces of gold—to buy this boat from a local fisherman. The fifteen-foot vessel had come with a rebuilt Kubota engine. It was making its first voyage to the ocean. Until that day, the boat had strictly been used to catch fish in the local rivers.

Ba tucked away all of his thoughts and worries in the back of his mind in order to keep himself from panicking. He had to focus on the task at hand and get everyone to Hong Kong.

As Ma stroked her belly, she, too, had her worries.

What if she went into labor on this boat? Would the baby be OK? Could they both survive? There were no doctors on board.

Ma had a healthy pregnancy so far. Her son or daughter was expected to arrive in a week, after they reached Hong Kong. However, if the baby decided to come early, while all were still at sea, the plan was for Ba and his sister Tam to do whatever was necessary to deliver the newborn. Ma prayed that the baby would come after they made it safely to shore.

They continued ahead in the ocean for the rest of the day, eating and drinking as little as they could.

As everyone finished their last shared ration for the day, there were loud splashes coming near the front of the boat.

"Look!" someone shouted.

Near the front of the boat, dolphins jumped from the depths of the sea, glinted in the sun, and splashed down in the water.

"Quynh, Nhu!" called Ma. She lifted Nhu and pointed toward the front of the boat.

The girls gasped and climbed over other people to see the dolphins. Two dolphins were jumping over each other like children. Both squeaked and creaked at each other.

The girls laughed and got wet from a final splash before the dolphins swam off.

The sun took its rest for the day, and the moon took its place in the sky.

Ahead in the distance stood a lighthouse. The tall white building was painted in white and red stripes. The light coming from it beamed out over the ocean, creating a path of light for other boats and ships that were navigating the black waters.

Ba steered the boat toward the lighthouse. The engine behind him sputtered and gasped again.

Ba hit it a couple of times. "Come on," he growled in annoyance. "Don't do this to me again. Come on, keep going."

The engine took its final breaths before dying.

Stranded at Sea

July 2, 1979

After enduring a sleepless night, Son and Ba, at the crack of dawn, set their eyes on getting the engine fixed as soon as they could.

During the night, the boat drifted in the darkness—and there was nothing Ba could do. He felt powerless, helpless that he had to wait until morning. All night, his thoughts poked and prodded him as he waited for the sun.

What if they couldn't get the engine fixed? Would they just continue drifting at sea? How far would they get? Were they all doomed to die on this boat?

After going over the engine for a couple of hours, the men stopped for the time being. No one knew how to fix it. Neither one had the tools or skills to do so. Ba never imagined that this could happen. He had prepared and planned for nearly everything but a broken engine. He felt foolish for not bringing anything in case the engine failed them *again*. It had just been fixed. Ba and Son had tested it several times before starting this journey. They wouldn't have relied on a faulty engine, risking their families. This was not supposed to happen.

Stranded in the South China Sea. Photo courtesy of BBC News

Ba sat back and looked at the never-ending sea. They were stranded. He felt he had let down his family and the others who trusted him, with his compass, to get them all to Hong Kong. He was now no longer in control; only the waves knew where they were taking them.

While the men were trying to fix the engine, Ma and the others prayed—prayed that God would give them hope again by having something as simple as an engine restart. But when the hours passed and the engine wasn't fixed, they felt lost in their unanswered prayers. Ma glanced around the boat, seeing others with their heads in their hands. Her gaze then turned to the wide-open ocean.

How would they survive stranded in the middle of the ocean? What would happen to the supplies? Would they get thirsty enough to try to drink the ocean water? What would they eat when they ran out of food?

The reality of it all was too much for some, who tried to bury their heads. Others tried to pray louder and longer, hoping something could be done.

But what could they do?

By the time the sun was at its highest point, some tried to shade themselves with their arms, blankets, or bags, and others went below. To seek the comfort of the ocean's coolness, others tied rope around their waists and jumped into the sea. When the comforting, cold water hit their burning skin, they felt refreshed.

Du, Ba's nineteen-year-old brother, was next to tie the rope around his waist and get into the water. He clung tightly to the boat, not wanting to let go. He leaned his head back and let the top of it get submerged. He sighed in relief.

Tam, Ba's twenty-four-year-old sister, made her way to Ma with a freshly dipped towel. She handed it to Ma, who thanked her and wiped the sweat off her forehead. Tam put her hand gently on Ma's stomach and asked, "Are you both doing OK?"

Ma put her hand on top of Tam's hand and, with a smile, said, "We're more than OK."

Quynh, sweat pooling on her tiny forehead, crawled to her father. She said, "Ba, it's too hot."

Ba looked around, trying to build something in his mind with all that they had on the boat. He eyed some blankets and the fishing poles—and an idea ignited. He and Son created shade by using fishing poles to prop up some blankets. Everyone sighed in relief once they were out of the sun's deadly rays. Quynh settled against her father and sighed deeply. "Thank you," she said.

The heat was oppressive, but having some shade helped block some of it.

As time passed, Ba sat there with his thoughts—ever buzzing about what they could do—when he felt a soft brush of wind against his cheeks. He lifted his hand, letting the wind graze him. He looked at the other unused blankets and bamboo sticks, and grabbed some fishing line.

He turned to his wife and said, "Help me with this." Ba grabbed a blanket, a sewing needle, and some fishing line, bringing all to Ma. She sewed the fishing line on the blanket while Ba made a hole in some plywood and stuck a bamboo stick in it. He tied the blanket onto the bamboo stick with the fishing line and knotted it on tight. Then, Ba tied the other end of the blanket to the propeller.

After an hour putting it together, Ba stood up proudly, and everyone on the boat clapped and cheered. Ma put her hand on her hard stomach as it cramped again. But just as quickly as the pain came, it disappeared. She bit her lip and looked at everyone's renewed hopeful faces. She didn't want to say anything yet. She still wasn't sure if this was labor pain or pain caused by stress.

The cheering from above alerted the girls, who poked their heads up from below the plywood.

"What happened?" asked Quynh.

Nhu took a finger from her mouth and pointed at the tied-up blanket. "What's that?"

Ma laughed and pulled her girls to her. "The engine died last night. So once we had light, Ba and I made a sail," Ma said. "Now the wind can take us to Hong Kong."

"Hong Kong?" asked Nhu.

"I thought we were going to America," said Quynh.

"We are," said Ma. "Our first stop is Hong Kong. And then hopefully from there we can take an airplane and fly to America."

Quynh and Nhu looked up to the sky in amazement. "Fly?" they asked in wonder.

A seagull cried above them.

Ma pointed to it. "Yes, we'll fly like a bird."

With the help of the wind, the boat was once again moving, but not as quickly as Ba would have wanted. He took out his trusty compass and made sure they continued forty-five degrees northeast, using a stick three yards long as a rudder to make sure they were going the right way.

Ba looked back. Vietnam was no longer in sight.

Battlefield

1970s

A t age eighteen, right after graduating high school, Ba wanted to serve his country, so he joined the army to fight against communism. For nine months, he trained at the Thu Duc Military Academy in Vietnam's capital, known then as Saigon. He and hundreds of other students graduated as officers and paratroopers. He had an active-duty obligation to serve for four years. Ba joined the Army of the Republic of Vietnam, fighting alongside the Americans to overthrow the communists.

Ba was assigned to the 2 Battalion of Red Beret, 24 Company. He was sent straight into the battlefield, into the wild jungles of central Vietnam in a region called Quang Tri.

Ba in the Army. Photo courtesy of Nguyen Family.

Ba tightly gripped his rifle in front of him and leaned his head back against the wall inside the helicopter. His green military helmet thumped against it. Next to him were other soldiers just like him, in their late teens, being sent out for the first time to fight at the front lines. The man to his left had his head bowed and was gripping a small wooden cross he kept in his pocket. The man to his right was still. He had his rifle steady, and his dark-brown eyes reflected determination. The man sitting across from Ba was sweating profusely, having to wipe his forehead constantly on his shoulder or with the back of his hand.

The helicopter they were in was flying across the sky, cutting through the heavy fog. Below them was a jungle, thick with green trees. Smoke floated in the distance, and the sounds of cannons were coming from nearby, right where the helicopter was taking them.

The helicopter began descending. A man at the front of the line, near the open door of the helicopter, stood and signaled for the rest of his men to do the same. The helicopter hovered above the ground, and each man jumped off. When it was Ba's turn, he took a deep breath and gasped when his feet touched the moss-covered ground. He followed the man in front of him, and all sought the cover of the trees. Once the last man jumped from the helicopter, two men carrying a stretcher hurried to the helicopter. A man with his head wrapped in a white bandage turning red cried as he was carried on the stretcher. The two men helped him get on the helicopter and stepped back as it rose and retreated to the nearest military hospital. Some of the men watched the helicopter with longing in their eyes, while others, including Ba, looked deep into the jungle, their hands ready on their weapons to use against the enemy.

On foot, they took off in single file, heading toward the sound of cannons, guns, and blood-curdling screams. The smell of smoke and sulfur filled the air and clung to the fog. They were ordered to get down to avoid being hit by bullets coming from the other side. As they got closer to battle, the fog subsided, revealing an intense, dangerous scene before them. One man was helping another as he limped his way past Ba and his unit. High-ranking men were shouting out orders as loud as they could over the chaos. Cannon fire flew back and forth across the jungle, dirt raining down upon them. Bullets sliced through the air, striking trees and flesh. Some men went down, while others continued firing back. Near the back of the chaos, where Ba and his unit had arrived, was a pile of dead bodies. Ba averted his gaze and focused on what lay ahead. The leader of his unit raised his rifle in the air. Others were encouraged by his outburst and took off to the front line. Ba raised his rifle in the air as well, and every step he took, he thought of his wife, Nga, whom he had married only a month before.

Fight for her and my country, he told himself.

Rain would pour for days, soaking into their clothes and turning the ground into mud. But whatever the weather, the fighting continued. Ba ignored the rain pouring down his back as he shot his rifle. The sound of the rain couldn't mask the continued gunfire and cannon blasts.

It was difficult to sleep. Being wet didn't help, but worse was the constant battle. Ba's eyes stung, but he was afraid that once he closed his eyes, he'd never open them again. The only time he was able to sleep was when he was partnered with someone and they took turns guarding over each other.

Once a week, Ba was able to step away from battle to see if Nga had written any letters to him. A man holding a burlap sack would call out names. Men would rush forward and grip the new letters tight against their chests. Some would kiss the envelopes as if they were a blessing.

One week, when Ba's name was called, his heart pounded and he smiled. Smiling was foreign there in the middle of war—it was difficult to smile about anything when death hung around like a dark shadow.

Ba went under a tree and heard birds calling out to one another in the distance. He opened the letter, and as he did, tears came to his eyes. He folded the letter away and put a hand over his mouth. He was going to be a father.

When he'd wanted to become a soldier, Ba knew he had to fight for his wife and his country. Now he had to fight for his unborn child and their future.

Ba tucked the letter into his front pocket—over his heart—then grabbed his rifle and went back into the fight, realizing how much more was at stake.

In the middle of the jungle in a continuous war, Ba counted down the days until Ma would give birth and he would be able to go home, even for a short period of time.

Men fell beside him and in front of him. Every night before taking a chance to sleep, he washed his blood-stained hands and found a tree trunk to sleep against. Bullets ricocheting off trees made him flinch in his sleep, and whenever cannon fire stirred him awake, Ba was too frightened to try to fall back asleep.

He always looked forward to those days he got letters from Nga. He would sniff the letter, bringing back intimate memories, and write letters back to her, saying how much he missed her and how he couldn't wait to hold their child. These constant thoughts of a blessing of a newborn kept him going and kept him sane through the hardships of war. Wanting to see and hold this child for the first time kept the darkness of war at bay. No matter how much death, blood, and fresh scars he saw, the thought of his child fought back and always won in the end. He wanted more than anything to fight for what this child deserved.

Ba thought all this violence and chaos had to mean something. It had to bring something good—something as good as a better future for this child.

Tiny fingers brushed along Ba's arm. He blinked and was brought back to being on the boat. He looked down and saw his first child gently brushing her fingers along the scar on his arm. Quynh had her head tilted to the side, looking at him with questions in her gaze.

"Sorry, Daughter," Ba said. "What did you say?"

Quynh looked down at the scar on his left arm. She put her small hand over it. "How did you get this? Does it hurt?"

Ba smiled and took her onto his lap, kissing her forehead. "It doesn't hurt. Hasn't in a long time."

"What happened?" asked Quynh. "How did you get that?"

Ba stared at his scar, bringing up buried memories. He hadn't looked at it in a long time. He didn't like the reminder that he could have lost his life and not been there to take his family to a better place.

"Ba?"

Ba squeezed his daughter. "I got hurt."

The sound of a gunshot pierced his mind. He could clearly hear the sound of a bullet hitting flesh.

"Someone hurt me. But I'm all right now," said Ba. He looked down at the scar. It was true that it had brought pain, but it had also brought him home just in time to witness the birth of Quynh.

Ba remembered that day vividly. He was luckier than most men. Lucky that when the bullet hit him, it wasn't a fatal shot. He could have lost his arm that day. He could have lost a whole lot more.

In the middle of the day, in the heat of battle, Ba fought along with other men beside him. There were screams of pain from those getting hurt and screams of triumph from those who hit their targets.

Getting ready to duck behind a tree, Ba was hit. The bullet hit his left arm and forced him to his knees. He looked down and saw a dark stain through his dark army-green shirt.

"Phu, are you hit?" shouted a man, who took a bag from his back and removed a shirt. He ripped off some fabric and tied it tightly around Ba's arm. Ba gasped at the pain.

"We need to keep pressure on it," said the man.

Cannon fire rammed into a nearby tree, exploding it. Ba and the man dropped onto the ground, covering their heads. Bark flew everywhere, little pieces raining down on them.

"We need to get you to the next chopper," said the man.

The man helped Ba stand, and both jogged to a group of other wounded men. Together they waited for the next helicopter. The man helped settle Ba onto the ground.

"How are you doing? Were you hit anywhere else?" The man looked over Ba, making sure there wasn't another wound.

"It feels like my whole arm is on fire," gasped Ba as he began to breathe hard. Next to him were other wounded men—men bleeding more heavily or who had lost limbs from cannon fire.

"OK, don't worry. Keep your eyes open," the man told Ba. "The next helicopter should be here soon. And when it arrives, I'll help you get on."

Just as the man finished speaking, the sound of helicopter blades drew closer and closer. Once the aircraft landed, Ba was lifted up and taken onto it.

"Heal that arm and kiss that pretty wife of yours," said the man.

Ba couldn't help but smile. "Thank you."

The man slapped his hand against the side of the helicopter, which then took off. Ba was taken to a nearby army clinic and was sent home to heal.

The timing couldn't have been better. His family celebrated his return, and Ba was able to be present for Quynh's birth.

Holding her in his arms, he felt himself slowly begin to heal from the gloom of war. The violence he had suffered and witnessed was snuffed out whenever he was in the presence of his daughter. She was his blooming flower in the darkness of war.

"Ba, what is that?"

Quynh's voice pulled him from the darkest parts of his memory. He saw her finger pointing out into the distance. Ba stood carefully, stretching his limbs. He put a hand over his eyes and looked to where she was pointing. It was a black dot.

"I'm not sure," he said.

They had been stranded for half a day and seen nothing but the endless ocean. That dot could be anything. But it was a welcome sight. Could it be a boat that would come to their rescue? Still, a feeling of dread crept up Ba's spine. Despite the heat of the day, a cool breeze washed over him. Could it be pirates? Were they about to be taken over by thieves?

Ba gripped the stick he used as a rudder and watched as the dot grew bigger and bigger. He sighed in relief when he saw it was too big to be a ship of pirates.

It was a naval ship.

Naval Ship

July 2, 1979

Were their prayers answered? Were they about to be saved? Ba directed the small fishing boat toward the dot. "We need to get closer and get their attention."

Son stood and made his way to the back of the boat, turning to everyone. "Raise your hands in the air and shout as loudly as you can. I'll let you know when to start."

Minutes later, he nodded. Everyone started shouting as loudly as they could. They waved their arms, mimicking the wind.

As the dot got closer, Ba realized that the vessel was indeed some type of naval ship. He recognized it as Chinese and knew that China was sympathetic to Vietnam's refugees. The ship honked, causing the children to jump and cover their ears. Nhu started crying. Ma took her in her lap and rocked her until her tears settled. Quynh sat next to Ma and put her hands over her ears, squeezing her eyes shut. Ba raised his arms in the air and shouted as loud as he could.

Ba could see men aboard the ship. Tiny as ants, they were proceeding with their usual working schedule. Not one man glanced down at their tiny boat—and if anyone did, none made an attempt to point them out.

The ship moved on, ignoring the tiny fishing boat and all seventeen passengers.

Once the ship passed them, everyone on the boat went silent, lowering their arms like deflated balloons. Son sat down next to Ba and sighed heavily. "Is that it? Are we destined to float endlessly and be ignored by passing ships?"

Ba shook his head in disbelief and looked out into the ocean. "But we can't give up. There must be more ships out there. All we need is one to stop for us."

Nhu looked up at Ma. "I want to go home."

Quynh lowered her hands and her bottom lip trembled. "Me too. And I'm hungry again. Why can't we eat more food?"

"America will be our new home," said Ma. "And we'll eat again soon. We're trying to save our food."

"But I want to eat now," said Nhu.

"When will we get to America?" asked Quynh.

"I know you two are hungry. How about you play a game, and after you're done, you can eat again," said Ma.

"When will we get to America?" asked Quynh again.

"It will take a while, my dear. Remember, we need to get to Hong Kong first," said Ma.

"When will we be in Hong Kong?"

Ma sighed. "Soon. In a few days. Why don't you play a game?"

Quynh crossed her arms over her chest, and Nhu copied her.

"I don't want to play a game. I'm hungry and want to go to Hong Kong now," said Quynh, pouting.

Ma sighed again, and Tam scooted over to them with random items in her hand. "How about we play with these?" she said. She held out the items as Nhu and Quynh looked. In her hands were a rock, a Vietnamese dong coin, and a piece of string. Nhu took the string and waved it in the air. Quynh took the rock and coin and pretended they were people.

Tam and Ma shared a smile.

As Tam watched her nieces play, she envied them. These girls would be able to adapt better than she would. They would be able to grasp the language better, and the American life. Tam had never learned how to speak English and never learned about America when she was at Da Lat University four years earlier. She wondered if she had what it would take to start all over again.

Tam's shoes echoed in the library at the university. Between classes, she loved to venture there, seeking the peace to study. The smell of old books brought her comfort.

Students were spread out through the library. Some sat at large wooden tables, with books piled up, as they scribbled down their notes. Others sought armchairs, resting their eyes or reading books for pleasure to take a break from studying.

Tam greeted the librarian and sought a table. As she set her book bag down, a loud siren sounded. She heard screams and shouts coming from outside the building. She picked up her book bag and, with the others in the library, looked out the windows. People were racing to their vehicles, jumping onto their bicycles, and running away.

"What's happening?" gasped the librarian.

A young man burst through the library doors, panting. "Saigon ... it's fallen."

Tam dropped her book bag on the floor. She watched as the other students ran out of the building and the librarian ran to the phone to make a call. Tam shook her head, picked up her bag and waited for the librarian to finish her call.

Is this it? she wondered. *Is this the end of Vietnam? Is this the end of my freedom? What is my future?*

The librarian hung up, tears falling down her cheeks. Then she hurried out of the library, leaving one of her shoes behind. Tam dialed a number and redialed it because she misdialed, her fingers shaking. She held the phone to her ear and waited.

A man answered. "Hello?"

"Father?"

"Tam, thank goodness," he said. "We've been calling your dorm. You need to come home now to Da Nang."

Her family lived north of her college, about four hundred miles away. Tam thought about her studies and her unfinished assignments. She had been studying science. She wasn't finished. Her life was just beginning.

"Tam?"

"Sorry. Yes, Father."

"You need to come home. It's not safe for you out there by yourself."

"OK, Father. I'm coming home." Tam hung up the phone and stared at it.

Outside, people were still screaming and shouting. She heard a large crash, which jolted her into action. She ran out of the building and saw a car mangled on the street.

Tam ran down the school path, ignoring other students, bumping into a few. She didn't stop until she made it to her dorm. She quickly packed what she could and took one more glance around the room. She had a feeling that she'd never return. She closed the door behind her with a soft click and began her way home.

She rushed from her dorm room to the street and flagged down a cab. After she got in, the driver weaved through traffic. The roads were bustling with activity and noise.

When they finally came to a bus station, she thanked the driver and handed him some money. She boarded a bus for the seventeen-hour ride home. After she arrived in Da Nang at eight the next morning, she finally made it to her childhood home.

On the first level was the family's tailor business. She expected to see her father dressed in his best suit and his hair combed back, not one strand out of place. Normally, there would be a line to enter the store. Locals praised it as the best shop to have your clothes repaired or altered.

Today, the door was locked and shut tight. The Closed sign stared out at her.

Tam made her way to the side of the building, where there was a set of stairs to the second level, where her family lived. She tried to open the door and frowned when she found that it was locked. She heard the doorknob twist and turn, then the door opened—and Tam was face-to-face with her mother.

Her mother smiled with tears in her eyes and hugged Tam. "I'm so relieved you made it here safely," she said. She pulled Tam into the house and locked the door behind her.

Tam set her book bag on the floor and collapsed onto a chair.

"Tam, what is it?"

"What's going to happen to us?" whispered Tam.

Her mother hunched over to hug Tam's head. "Don't you worry, my daughter. You're with your family now. We'll look after you."

"What will happen to me?" asked Tam, tears filling her eyes.

Tam's mother knelt down and put Tam's face in her hands. "Nothing will happen to you. Your father and siblings will always look after you."

"You promise?"

"I promise. Even though the communists have taken over, as a family, we'll continue to keep our business open."

Tam heard Nhu squeal in delight as she played with her string. Nhu would let it go and have the wind carry it. Then she'd clap her hands and do it all over again. Tam looked over to her brother, Phu. He held his gaze to the never-ending sea—waiting for another ship to come. She made her way over to him and grasped his hands.

"Tam?" he said.

Tears came into her eyes. "Thank you, Brother. Thank you," she said, burying her head into his shoulder. He wrapped an arm around her.

"You never have to thank me, Tam. We're family. We'll always look out for one another."

Throughout the day, other big ships of all shapes and sizes passed, honking their loud horns and scaring the children. Everyone on the fishing boat would raise their arms in the air and shout. But every ship passed them. Not one slowed down. Not one glanced at such a tiny boat overflowing with people. Not one stopped to help them.

As everyone was beginning to lose hope—shouting less and not raising their arms whenever another big ship was spotted—Son's eyes lit up with an idea. "I know what to do," he said.

He grabbed a towel and held it over the water to pour some oil over it. He grabbed a match and scraped it on a piece of plywood. The match ignited. Son then lit the towel. As a big ship got closer, Son waved the flaming towel in the air, hollering as loud as he could. Inspired, those on the fishing boat gathered the last of their strength, raised their arms, and yelled out as loud as they could one last time.

Some men on the passing ship looked down, trying to see where the fire was coming from. The towel was getting hot in Son's hands, and the whole thing was almost consumed by the flames. Son threw it, and it landed on the water with a hiss. It sizzled and went out, black as everyone's mood on the boat. Son looked up at the ship and, along with the others, watched it pass them by.

Their tiny boat rocked them as if the ocean itself was trying to comfort those in the boat. Their throats were dry and coarse. Their arms were tired, as were their spirits.

No one stopped for the small fishing boat that day. And as other big ships came, no one had the heart to shout or raise their arms. Their faith was extinguished like the flaming towel that Son had tossed into the ocean.

Stranded at Sea. Photo courtesy of BBC News.

Those not lucky enough to get some shade had sore, red skin. Some even had blisters.

Ba began to worry more about the water than the food. He was hoping that the water would last long enough for someone to come save them, fix their engine, and provide them with more food and water.

Ma rubbed her belly absentmindedly. She looked around at her family's frowns and desperately wanted to wipe them away. But what could she say or do? She gasped when she felt a strong cramp and hugged her stomach.

Tam looked at her with wide eyes. "Is it time?" she asked.

Ma shook her head. "It's probably nothing. I'm just stressed."

Tam sat next to Ma. "Stress can bring a baby early."

Ma licked her lips and rubbed her belly. "But the baby is supposed to come next week. It's not supposed to come now."

Tam put a hand on Ma's belly. "The baby will come when it's ready."

"I'm sure it's nothing," said Ma, smiling.

"Phu and I are here for you and the baby. We're going to do our best. As will you."

Ma's bottom lip trembled, and she hugged Tam. "I'm scared."

Tam hugged her back. "Don't be. God is with you and your baby. He'll protect you both. You'll see."

As everyone settled in for the night, Quynh snuggled up next to her father. He stroked her hair to help her fall asleep.

"Ba?"

"Yes, Quynh?"

"Why didn't the ships stop for us?"

Ba sighed heavily, thinking carefully about his next words. "Either they didn't see us or they didn't want to stop."

Quynh lifted her head. "But why?"

Ba chuckled. "Get some sleep. We have another long day at sea."

Quynh shut her eyes and, with the help of the ocean rocking the boat, fell asleep in no time.

Ba looked up at the stars as Quynh's question ran through his head. He didn't want to dwell on that question. He always answered with, "We'll try the next one. Another ship will come and they'll save us." But no ship ever did.

The naval ships were accustomed to seeing many boats overstuffed with people going across the South China Sea. Ba's boat wasn't the first to escape Vietnam. There were many boats that left before them and many that continued to leave Vietnam after. It wasn't the naval ships' duty to help every boat they came across.

Ba did his best to try to fall asleep, trying to think of what was waiting for them in Hong Kong and in America, not what was waiting on the ocean or beneath them in the depths.

Ma was too restless to close her eyes and try to fall asleep. She put her hand on her belly. Tears pricked her eyes as she thought about her own mother, someone she hadn't seen in a long time. She thought back to the day when she had said goodbye to her parents—the day she and her daughters had tried to escape Vietnam the first time.

Grandparents Escape

April 1975

S aigon had fallen. The communists seized the capital city. The war was lost in the South; the communists had won. A panic spread through the city.

In the chaos, Ma's parents, with the last of their gold, bought a boat for themselves and their children. Her father wanted a good-sized boat to flee the country, taking as many family members as he could.

At this time, Ma and her two daughters lived with her parents while Ba was at war. Ma's mother knocked on her bedroom door early one day.

"Nga, your father got a different boat this time. And this time, we can make it. Please, I beg of you. Come with us. Come before it is too late," said Bà Ngoại (which means "maternal grandmother" in Vietnamese).

Ma fiddled with her wedding ring. She looked down at it, and Bà Ngoại put her hand on it. "I'm sorry, dear. Your husband is a brave man. But this is what he would have wanted for you and for your children. He joined the army to fight against communism, to fight against what this country has become. We lost."

Ma's eyes filled with tears. Since communism had taken over, she had never heard from Ba, never heard of his whereabouts, and never even heard if he was still alive. It had been months of silence.

Bà Ngoại tightened her grip and wiped away Ma's tears. "Please, escape with us. I can't leave you three behind. Give your children a better life. A life they deserve and can't get here."

Ma sniffled and took a deep breath. "OK, Mother. We'll go with you."

Bà Ngoại sighed in relief and hugged Ma tight. "Thank you. Thank you." She let go. "We leave in three weeks."

They used that time to make last-minute preparations for the journey ahead. They hoped for calm seas—seas that would take them to a refugee camp in Singapore. Ma's father, Ông Ngoại, heard rumors that hundreds of others who had fled safely to Singapore were waiting to resettle in America. He hoped to follow that same path. They would go south, and the journey would be roughly six hundred miles. Ông Ngoại knew that he and his family would never return. This was it.

When it was time to leave, Ma took the girls and headed to the ocean shore. It was in the early hours, before the sun was even awake.

Ma watched as her seven siblings walked in small groups to the boat. After waiting a couple of minutes, Ma and the girls made their way, too. Her father helped her and the girls aboard. "Go ahead and find a place to lie down," he said.

On this boat, there was a cooking area. Here they stored bags of rice, beans, and dry fish. Ma and the girls lay next to the bags of food and waited for the rest of their relatives to board the boat.

Those on board went below or covered themselves with blankets or fishing nets.

At the docks, Ma saw others trying to flee as well. Boats were coming and going. Engines were fired up and people rushed their families on board while taking as many supplies as they could. Bà Ngoại had sewn pieces of gold inside her children's clothes. Ma had a gold coin stashed in her shirt.

During the entire ride out to the ocean, Ma kept looking back. Ba wasn't with her. She didn't know what had happened to him and desperately wanted to know. She needed answers. They had been married for two and a half years and were blessed with two daughters.

Each day, she worried and felt the weight on her shoulders get heavier and heavier. Communism was spreading, and she had no word on what had happened to her husband. Was he being held captive? Or did the communists take his life for fighting against them?

The ocean was unkind. The waves slamming against the boat made everyone sick. The vomit being spewed on the floor would be washed away by waves that rained down on them.

Ma and her children were weak—weak from being unable to keep food in their bellies and weak from the ocean waves.

Nhu cried throughout the day and into the night. Ma couldn't say or do anything to soothe her tears.

Ma, whose heart ached, put a hand over her own mouth to stifle her crying. She realized she couldn't do this. She looked back at the shore and felt a giant throb in her chest. She looked down at her children and saw their dad in their faces. Ma then realized that she couldn't leave her husband behind, not without knowing his whereabouts.

"Take us back," she cried.

"What?" asked Ông Ngoại.

Ma put a hand on her heart and rubbed her chest. "Take us back. Please, Father. I can't leave without my husband."

"But, but ..." began Bà Ngoại.

Ông Ngoại tightened his grip on the steering wheel. Leave his eldest daughter behind? The father in him refused. He would see this through. He would get all of his children to safety in another country.

"And your granddaughter, she's too sick," Ma said. "She keeps heaving and is getting weaker. She can't make this trip." Ma put a hand on his arm gently. "Father, I know you don't want to leave us behind. I know it goes against everything you are as a father. But I am a parent, too. I can't bear to see Nhu suffer anymore. I'm also a wife. I can't leave Phu behind. I can't leave without knowing what happened to him."

Ông Ngoại put a hand over hers. "He's your family now." He squeezed her hand. "Are you sure this is what you really want?"

Ma nodded, tears flowing down her cheeks. "Yes. We can't do this. Phu should be here, he should be here with us, trying to escape. Seeking out a better life. I can't start that without him."

Ông Ngoại nodded with a heavy heart. His eldest wasn't a little girl anymore. She was building a life with her husband and two young kids. "If that's what you wish."

Bà Ngoại's heart broke as the boat was turned around.

It took a day and a half to get back to the shores of Vung Tau, still bustling with people getting their boats ready to venture into the ocean and leave Vietnam.

This was the most pain Bà Ngoại had ever felt in her life. She wanted all eight of her children with her. But she had to let her oldest one go.

Ông Ngoại steered the boat toward the docks. He wrapped his arms around his daughter and two grandchildren. "Be safe. I pray Phu gets brought back to you."

Ma kissed her father's cheek. "Thank you."

Bà Ngoại accompanied her daughter and two granddaughters off the boat. She hugged each one tightly and breathed in their scent.

Bà Ngoại had tears falling down her cheeks. Her heart was filled with uncertainty. Was this the last time she would see them? Was this the last time she would speak to them? What if they never escaped Vietnam? Or if they did, how far would they make it?

"Are you sure you won't come with us?" pleaded Bà Ngoại. "It's not safe here. Especially for your children."

Ma wiped her mother's tears. "I can't. I can't leave without my husband. Not without knowing what happened to him."

"Go stay with your aunt for a while," said Bà Ngoại, forcing a smile.

Bà Ngoại, her hands shaking, let go of Ma and went back on the boat. She looked back and kept looking until she couldn't see them on the shore anymore. She found a spot to sit on the boat and wept. No one could console her.

Back on shore, Ma watched the boat get smaller and smaller until it was a black dot. As she watched her family sail away, her brain was flooded with memories of the life her parents had created in Vietnam. This was one of the hardest decisions she had ever had to make. She didn't know if she would ever see her family again. What if this was her last image of her family? What if this was their final goodbye?

She looked down at her ring. With this ring, she had made a promise to her husband and his family. She wouldn't leave this country without him. She would wait for word.

"This isn't goodbye," whispered Ma. She bowed her head and prayed. Prayed for her family's safe journey across the sea and their journey to America. And lastly, she prayed for the safe return of her husband.

Ma made herself turn away from the ocean and headed to her aunt's house, holding hands with her children. Her eyes were filled with tears, but she held no regret. She felt this was the right decision for herself and her family.

As Ma looked at Nhu and Quynh sleeping peacefully next to their dad on the fishing boat, the pain she had buried that day resurfaced. It had been one of the hardest days of her life.

Ma and her girls had stayed with her aunt for a while and eventually moved in with Ba's family. Several months passed before Ma received word that her family had made it to America.

From her spot toward the back of the boat, she looked across the vast ocean and thought of her mother, father, and siblings. She hoped she would see them again. Hoped that they could be a family again in America. Every day that passed was another day closer to being reunited with them. It had been too long.

Ma gasped when she felt a sharp pain come from her belly. She put both hands on her stomach and took a deep breath. The pain came again, and Ma whimpered.

Ba woke to the sound of gasping and heavy breathing. He grabbed the flashlight and shined it at where the noise was coming from.

Ma was sitting up, her hands on her stomach and sweat starting to build on her forehead. Ba went down next to her and put an arm around her.

"Are you OK?" he asked.

She gasped and put a hand on her belly. The pain was getting worse. Ba pulled back and looked at her. "What? What happened now?"

"The baby's coming," she said.

The Birth

July 3, 1979

I t was pitch black. The new moon didn't offer any light; the only light source came from a flashlight.

Ba squeezed Ma's shoulder reassuringly. "Let's try to make it to sunrise so that we have more light," he said.

Ma nodded and rubbed her stomach.

Ba went to Tam and woke her up by shaking her shoulder. "Tam," he said.

She blinked her heavy eyes open. "What is it?" she croaked.

"It's Nga. She's having pains. Birth pains. She's going to have the baby."

Tam woke from his words, her eyes no longer heavy, and followed Ba to the back of the boat.

Du was toward the front of the boat, lying on the wooden planks. He had fallen asleep looking at the stars. He woke up to the sound of Nga's heavy breathing. He kept lying there, afraid to move. He didn't want to peek and see how they were doing. He closed his eyes and pretended to be asleep. But his ears heard everything.

Tam sat beside Ma and grasped her hand, Ma's lifeline through the pain. "It'll be OK, Nga. I'm here. Phu's here, we're all here for you," said Tam.

All of a sudden, there was a bird cry and the boat rocked. Ma looked and saw a big black bird, possibly a pelican, perched on the edge of the boat. It ruffled its feathers and flapped its wings. Ma forgot about the pain and was awed by the bird. *Where did it come from?* Ma wondered. *How did it stray so far from land to be here, in the middle of the sea?*

When the bird flapped its wings, the wind it created cooled off Ma and the others surrounding her. The bird cried out one final time, stretched its wings, and took off, blending into the darkness. Once the bird left, Ma knew she could do this. She wasn't alone in this and knew everything was going to be OK. With a sense of relief, she took the bird as a sign from God to help her with the labor.

She closed her eyes and prayed. Prayed for God to give her strength and safety for herself and, most important, for her baby.

Ba and Tam were feeling the effect of the ocean as it rocked the boat and their stomachs. Gravity was no more. Their vision spun, and their stomachs knotted up and threatened to throw up what little they contained. The only thing that helped was the reassuring wind, blowing on their hot and sweaty skin. They tried to take deep breaths, inhaling the ocean and the cool breeze. Tam and Ba had to be strong for Ma and did their best to ignore their own nausea.

Ma gripped Tam's hand tight as her contractions started. Ba grabbed another flashlight, his hands shaking. He looked to his friend Son, who was still sleeping.

"We're going to need more help," whispered Ba. "Son, Son, wake up."

Son sat up fast and looked at the scene before him. Tam was taking out the supplies to get ready for the baby. She took out scissors, a knife, and some baby blankets. She looked deeper into the bag and frowned. She looked up at Ba and Son.

"What happened to the spool of thread?"

Son looked in the bag and had no luck. "We must have lost it."

Tam took the bag and pulled out a towel. "We'll need something to sew with."

"Fishing line," suggested Ba.

Son set down the bag and went to get some fishing line. When he returned, Tam handed Son a towel.

"Get ready to hold the baby," said Tam.

As Ba held the flashlights, their beams of light were bouncing all over the place. Tam put a hand on his leg, and he instantly stilled.

She offered him a smile and then turned to Ma. "OK, Nga. Time to push." Tam was reassuring and encouraging Ma.

"You're doing great, Nga."

"Keep pushing, Nga."

"The baby's almost here."

Ma's screams ran over the ocean, and the waves calmed. Some people on the boat awakened to her cries. They saw the scene before them. Some looked away—out of respect and privacy—while the women smiled and encouraged Ma, whispering prayers her way.

With one final cry from Ma and a hard hand squeeze, the baby was born. Son wrapped a towel around the newborn, who then started to cry.

Ba looked over Son's shoulder and then down at Ma. "It's a girl," he said, tears coming to his eyes.

Tam wiped the sweat from Ma's forehead and hugged her.

Ma cried out, "A girl!"

Tam took the flashlights from Ba and gestured for him to go down to Ma.

He kissed Nga and hugged her. "It's a girl," he breathed into her hair.

Ma smiled, and Ba pulled back. He grabbed the scissors and cut the umbilical cord with it. "Tam, hand me the fishing line," he said.

Ma laid her head back, feeling exhausted and seasick.

Tam, with steady hands, gave Ba the fishing line, and he sewed up what was left of the umbilical cord at the baby's belly button.

Son held the baby and gently rocked her. "Now what?"

Tam shined a flashlight on the water. "We have to clean her." She set the flashlights down. "I'll help."

53

They dipped the towels in the ocean and used them to gently wipe the baby, removing all the blood and other fluids.

After they cleaned her, Tam got the blanket, and Son wrapped the baby in it.

Son looked down at the baby, whose brown eyes were fluttering. He smiled down at her. "Hi, little one."

Tam, turning to Ma, said, "We have to push out the rest of the placenta. Phu, push on her stomach."

Tam took the baby from Son, who then helped Ba. Ba pushed on Ma's stomach—and out came the placenta. Son picked it up, all bloody. "What do I do with it?" he asked.

"Just toss it in the ocean," Ba said with a shrug. And Son did.

Tam brought the baby to Ba. "Congratulations," Tam said to him.

Ba smiled down at his baby girl. Tam knelt next to Ma and began to clean the blood and other fluids from Ma as best as she could while holding a flashlight.

Once Tam finished cleaning her up, Ma held out her arms. "The baby, where is she?"

"Right here," said Ba.

Ba handed the crying baby to Ma, who immediately began breastfeeding her. As she fed the baby, Ba, Tam, and Son leaned over the boat and washed their hands and arms with ocean water.

With tears in her eyes, Ma gazed down at the baby. "My little miracle." She looked up into the sky. "Thank you, God."

When daylight filled their world again, Ma needed to finish cleaning herself up. She didn't know how to swim, so Ba tied a rope around her waist and helped her into the ocean. Ma gripped the side of the boat and sighed in relief, the ocean's coolness refreshing her skin.

After Ma cleaned herself, Ba helped her back on the boat and got her dressed. Ma sat down, her limbs shaking. Tam handed her the baby.

"Have you thought of a name?" asked Tam.

Ma opened her mouth but turned to see Quynh climbing toward them. Quynh gasped and looked at her baby sister.

"She's so pretty," said Quynh. She stroked the baby's soft head. "What's her name?"

Ma kissed her baby's forehead and said, "Dai Duong."

Dai Duong comes into the World. Photo courtesy of BBC News.

"Hi, Dai Duong," whispered Quynh. "What does Dai Duong mean?"

Ba sat down and looked at his family with proud eyes. "It means grand ocean."

Quynh lifted her eyes up at the endless sea around them. "Grand ocean," she repeated. She held out her hands. "Can I hold her?"

Ma handed Dai Duong to Quynh. "Gently now. Be careful of her head."

Tam sat behind Quynh as she held Dai Duong. Quynh smiled and kissed her new sister's head. When Dai Duong, whose eyes were closed, felt the kiss, a little smile appeared on her face.

As everyone else woke up, they were excited and filled with joy at the coming of a new life. All were hoping that the baby's arrival was a sign that they would be rescued, that someone would come save them. They took the birth as a sign that God would help see them through this. But before they could restart their lives, they needed to reach Hong Kong.

Ba kept their boat at forty-five degrees northeast, his course set for Hong Kong. For the rest of the day they all rested on their boat—eating and drinking as little as possible, trying to save as much as they could.

The next day, the sun was unkind. Its rays were hot, and all on the boat needed to cool off. Everyone took turns tying rope around their waists and jumping into the ocean. When they were in the water, they would hold on to the boat and rinse themselves off in the cool water.

On the boat, Nhu and Quynh began to cry.

Tam went to them. "What is it, girls?"

"We're so thirsty," cried Quynh.

Nhu sniffled and wiped her snot and tears on her arm.

Tam wiped Nhu's arm clean and hugged the children. "I know. We all are. But don't worry. A boat will come help us and give us more water to drink."

She rocked the children along with the boat and helped soothe them to sleep.

Their nap didn't last long, for another ship was spotted in the distance. Its horn woke the girls up.

Ba and Son gave each other a look. Ba turned his eyes to his family.

Ma was rocking a startled Dai Duong, and Tam was holding Quynh and Nhu, trying to get them to sleep again. Dai Duong had begun crying when the loud ship honked its horn.

Ba turned back to Son. "Let's try again," he said.

Son looked at the newborn baby and also looked at his own family. He nodded, and he and Ba stood up.

"For our families," said Son.

They raised their arms in the air and shouted as loud as they could. This was their second day stranded out at sea. Ba and Son hoped the incoming naval ship would react differently than all the other vessels that had passed them. Ba hoped the ship would stop next to their boat, lower a rope, and pull them all aboard. They would be able to eat until their stomachs were full and drink to their hearts' content. This ship had to stop, had to save them. Would this be the ship that finally rescued them?

Oil Rig

July 4, 1979

As the ship passed them, Ba and Son lowered their arms. They had tried getting its attention, but it just continued on its course, not caring to stop for the little fishing boat.

Ba sat down heavily, careful not to show his disappointment. He took out a cigarette and puffed out his frustration. He couldn't give up. There was nothing else to do but keep trying.

Throughout that hot, humid day, Son and Ba tried to get the attention of every passing boat. They'd shout as loud as they could and wave their arms in the air.

The wind, thankfully, was still pushing them along, but it still wasn't enough. They needed help. They needed only one of these boats to stop to help fix their engine.

Their food and water were running low. Everyone would take only a spoonful of water and a bit of food.

Ba relied on smoking to keep his hunger at bay. He puffed his cigarettes and drank rice wine. He would pass the bottle to Son, and both savored the vinegary, spicy, caramel-like taste. It soothed their throats as it went down and helped quench their thirst for water.

When Son finished taking some sips of rice wine, he glanced at Ba's family. Watching them, he couldn't help but think of the family he had left behind. He had been able to bring on the boat his two younger brothers, two nephews, and two family friends. But his heart ached for the three people he was missing the most: his pregnant wife and two young children. His wife had been too scared to try to make the journey—and Son shared her fear. He, too, believed that the journey was too dangerous for them. So he made one of the most difficult decisions in his life: he left them behind. He made the massive sacrifice of going on without his family. They were the only thing driving him to the end goal of finding a new home. He promised to make contact with them as soon as he reached Hong Kong and got resettled.

Son finished off his rice wine and handed Ba back the glass. "Do you remember when we first met?" he asked.

Ba grinned and took Son's glass. "I do. We've known each other a long time. Since we were their age." He nodded toward Quynh and Nhu.

"We did practically everything together," said Son, whose grin slowly disappeared. "I'm sorry, though, that I wasn't with you at camp."

Ba squeezed Son's shoulder. "Come on, now. You became a teacher. That's respectable."

"I didn't like it," said Son. "Hated what I had to teach. Thought it was all wrong, praising communism like that."

"You did what you had to do, Son. Trust me, I'm glad you weren't there with me. The camps have a dark place in my memories. You don't need those to plague you."

Son cracked a smile. "I'm glad you were able to get out and are here with us today. Without you, none of this," said Son, sweeping his arm around, pointing at the boat and everyone on board. "None of this would have happened."

Ba refilled their empty glasses, and they clinked them. "To our great escape," said Ba.

To pass the time, Nhu grasped a handful of Quynh's hair and played with it.

Ma, who was breastfeeding Dai Duong, sat next to Quynh. She stroked Quynh's cheek. "How about you and Nhu sing a song for your baby sister, Dai Duong?"

Quynh looked up at Nhu, and both began to sing. "One shining star. Two stars shining. Three shining stars, shining countless golden glitters. There we have four stars shining. There we have five stars shining. There we have six stars shining in the sky."

"Sing again," cooed Ma. "And use your fingers to count."

As Quynh and Nhu sang again, they held up their fingers all the way to six.

When they finished singing, others nearby clapped. They were thankful for the welcome distraction.

"You girls sing beautifully," someone said. "Go on, sing something else."

The girls continued singing, and Ba stood up, squinting his eyes toward the distance. He saw a dot, which he thought was a big ship. Ba made sure their boat stayed its course toward the dot.

The girls stopped singing and Quynh gagged. Tam quickly went to her and held her as she threw up over the side of the boat.

When Quynh finished, Tam washed her face off with ocean water and encouraged her to rinse her mouth. Quynh began crying and Tam held her close. She scooped some ocean water into her hands and poured it on Quynh's forehead to try to cool her off.

"I don't feel good," cried Quynh.

"It will pass," said Tam. "We all get seasick because of the motion. Close your eyes and take deep breaths."

Quynh was able to go to sleep, and, as the sun went down, everyone turned quiet early, tired from the heat's strength. Ba and Son eyed the dot, which was getting bigger as they were heading closer to it.

By nightfall, as they got closer to the dot, they saw lots of lights coming from something. When another hour had passed, they finally were able to figure out where all those lights were coming from: the boat had made it to a giant oil rig. There was a canoe tied to it, and surrounding the contraption were buoys.

The waves got rough, as if the ocean was all riled up. But Son and Ba did not let the ocean dampen their spirits.

Ba smiled at Son. "We're going to live."

Son dropped his smile. "What if it's a communist oil rig?"

Ba shook his head. "Doesn't matter. Our families will live. Perhaps we get thrown back in jail," he began. He put a hand on Son's shoulder. "But our families get to live. There must be someone up there to help us." Ba let him go and grabbed a rope on their boat. "Get us close, Son."

Son steered the boat closer to the oil rig, and the wind helped move it faster. The waves continued rocking the boat. This woke up almost all the adults, but the children continued sleeping. At their age, they were hard to wake up once they had passed out.

"Careful, Son, we don't want to slam up against the rig," said Ba.

He worried that they would hit the buoys too hard. He didn't want their boat to be damaged—or worse, his family be tossed into the waves and, since none of them could swim, drown.

Ba turned to Thong, one of Son's relatives, who was wide awake and staring up at the oil rig in awe. "Thong, you see that ladder? Do you think you can jump to it?" asked Ba. "Then I'll toss you this rope and you tie it on."

Thong nodded and leaned over the boat. As Son got their boat close, Thong leapt over the water and grabbed the ladder. His feet slipped, but the strength in his arms held him. He turned to Ba, who threw him the rope. Thong tied the rope tight around the ladder.

The waves were getting rougher and water was pouring into the boat. Everyone now was awake and shaking from the cold.

Thong got back on the boat, and Ba stood. "I'm going to see if I can check things out."

Son nodded and watched Ba climb the ladder.

As Ba got closer to the main deck of the oil rig, he could hear men speaking Chinese. He paused and sighed in relief that they weren't speaking Vietnamese. He didn't want to be taken back to Vietnam. He listened for a tiny bit, testing the little Chinese he knew. Ba knew more English than Chinese, having learned it during the war when he was fighting alongside American soldiers against the communists. He went up one more step and shouted in English, "Hello!"

Small Boat in a Big Sea. Photo Courtesy of BBC News.

He heard footsteps, and a bright white light shined down on their tiny boat.

"Water, water!" shouted Ba in English.

"When it's sunrise, we'll talk," the men shouted back in Chinese.

Ba hung his head and climbed back down the ladder. When he got back on the boat, the light got switched off.

"Well? What happened?" asked Son.

"They said they'll talk with us at sunrise," said Ba.

All cast their eyes down and did their best to sleep until morning. But their thoughts raced and kept them awake.

"What if they take us back to Vietnam?" asked Du, hoping someone could answer him. "I can't go back to jail. I can't." His voice cracked.

Hearing his brother's anguish, Ba put a hand on his shoulder. "It's OK," said Ba. "If they take us to Vietnam, at least we all are alive. Try and get some sleep."

Du shook his head. "You're OK going back, back to those so-called reeducation camps? They held you captive for three years."

Ba tried not to shiver from Du's words.

In Vietnam, reeducation camps spread throughout the land when the communists won. It was said these camps were supposed to help reeducate people—those who fought against them—to help them learn about the new government and a new way of life. But they were far from educational. They were prison camps where men could spend ten years away from their families and were put to hard labor.

"I know it's hard for you to understand, but I have children and a wife who depend on me," said Ba. "And I'd rather be alive in a reeducation camp or jail knowing they're safe."

"But you have more at stake than I do," said Du. "I don't have a wife or kids." He shook off Ba's hand and moved to the front of the boat.

Ba watched his brother move in the darkness and lowered his hand to his side. His brother was right. The whole time Ba had been in the reeducation camps, the thoughts of his wife and girls had gotten him through those dark days. What did Du have? Their parents? Their siblings? What did he have to help him continue the fight?

"Your life and future, Du," Ba called out in the dark. He waited for a response, staring out into the dark. When he heard nothing, he went to find a spot next to his girls to sleep.

Du tossed and turned under the deck, where he was trying to sleep. His last conversation with his brother was still fresh in his mind. He couldn't believe Phu wouldn't mind going back to those reeducation camps. While Phu was imprisoned at those camps, Du had been placed in jail.

Just over a year earlier, at age eighteen, Du had been stripped of his freedom. He and two other brothers had planned to escape Vietnam, but they were caught by the local police and thrown in jail.

Every day, from a young age, he'd sought the outdoors, a tennis racket in one hand. His father not only owned a tailor business but was also quite an athlete. A winner of many tournaments, he was greatly admired. When Du was finally old enough, his father placed a tennis racket in his hands and showed him how to play.

But in jail, he lost such a privilege. He couldn't go outside and feel the wind on his face. He couldn't grasp a racket and swing. He was stuck in a cell for three weeks. He had never feared for his life more than he did during that time. But he did his best to not show his weakness and not be intimidated.

His mother finally came to bail him out, bringing two to three ounces of gold with her. In those weeks, she thought her sons had escaped. She had just heard the news that they were in jail. So, she scraped up some gold and was determined to get Du out first.

On the day of his release, he hugged her tight and she hummed softly to him.

"I didn't know you were here. I'm so sorry, Son."

"It's all right, Ma. It's in the past." He let her go and offered his arm. "Let's get out of here and go home."

As they walked away, his mother looked back, but Du refused to do so. He never wanted to see that place again or set foot near a jail again. He wouldn't be caught trying to escape again.

Just a few days before Du found himself stranded at sea on Ba and Son's fishing boat, he had been sleeping peacefully at home. Thoughts of trying to escape had left him. He wouldn't try again. He was grateful for his freedom and being able to do what he wanted when he wanted. For the majority of his new days of freedom, he played tennis and enjoyed what nature had to give him.

But that morning, his mother had woken him up, shaking his shoulder. "Du, wake up. Get up."

Du stretched in his bed. "What is it, Ma?"

She began throwing clothing onto his bed. "You need to go with Tam, now. Go to the docks. Escape with your siblings."

Du quickly sat up in bed, with his eyes wide. "Escape?"

"That's what I said." She tried to pull him out of bed, but he wouldn't budge. "Did you hear me? You have to hurry, Du."

"But what if we get caught?" Du said, shivering. "I can't go back to jail."

"You won't," she said. With the last of her strength, she pulled him out of bed. "Get dressed. Escape with Tam and Phu. Don't look back. Your freedom depends on this."

Du tugged on a shirt and zipped up his pants. "And you?"

"I'm staying."

"But—"

"No buts. Get going." She dragged him outside, where Tam was waiting. Their mother hugged Du to her chest. "You and your siblings were meant to have a better life than me. That's what any parent would want for their children." She kissed his cheek and pushed him to his sister. "Go. Hurry."

She watched her children disappear into the darkness and cried. She wiped away her tears and prayed that they would look after one another.

Du shoved the heel of his hands into his eyes to stop himself from crying. He missed his family and his home. He didn't know what it would be like to live in America. He knew freedom was there, but would the country welcome him? He wanted to feel a part of something; he didn't want to be an outcast. Also, he didn't want to let his parents down. They brought him into this world with his siblings to have a better life than they had. But how could he if they were caught again?

Du looked up at the oil rig. The lights had been shut off for a while now, and he didn't see any men. He didn't like knowing that the fate of his freedom was in their hands.

In the late night, Son and Ba were wakened by water at the bottom of their boat.

"Use anything you can to try to get it out," said Ba.

The men on the boat tried to get the water out with their hands or the bowls that once held food. But it was no use. Despite how much they tried to remove the water, it seemed to stay at the same depth. Their futile efforts were like trying to fight back against the wind—nothing seemed to help. The men paused. They would try again later; for now, sleep called out to them. Du slept above on the wooden planks, while Ba took first watch. Du watched Ba's cigarette flicker like a tiny lantern in the darkness.

Below, people squirmed. Water got into the girls' clothes. Ma and Tam shivered against the cold. Eventually, everyone took turns sleeping on the wooden planks so that no one would sleep soaked to the bone.

By sunrise, workers in bright-orange jumpsuits were looking down at the little boat tied to their oil rig. Each man was aiming his gun at the boat. They were on the rig's main deck, at least two hundred feet above the boat. The distance was too far to yell back and forth.

As Ba smoked a cigarette, Son pointed up. "What's that?" he asked.

Ba looked up and saw something being lowered to them. It was a basket. When it reached them, Son untied it and smiled. "It's food and water," he said.

The men above had sent down fried Chinese doughnuts, tangerines, and canned fruit with a can opener.

As Son passed the food and water to everyone, Ba found a note the workers had written in English, along with pen and paper in the basket. Ba read the note:

You have to leave. This is a restricted area.

Ba wrote the following reply:

We need water and food. Our engine broke. Help us get to Hong Kong.

Ba returned the paper and pen to the basket and pulled on it. The men above lifted the basket.

Ba turned to Ma, who was holding Dai Duong. "Show them we have a baby."

Ma lifted up Dai Duong in the air. The workers took out their binoculars, pointed down at the baby, and put their guns away. Ma put the baby back down as a couple of workers climbed down with eight oars.

One handed Ba an oar and said, "Row away."

"Row where?" asked Ba.

"You have to leave," the worker said. "This is a restricted area. No one is allowed here."

"We can't. We need food and water. Our engine broke," said Ba.

"OK, stay there," said the worker.

The two workers went back up the ladder.

After some minutes had passed, they sent down another basket filled with more food. Inside were jars of orange slices, two boxes of cereal, and some crackers.

Looking at the bottom of the cereal box, Ba saw that it had been made in the United States. Ba smiled, seeing this as a good sign that the workers above were on good terms with America.

Once they got everything out of the basket, two workers came down and took a look at their engine.

When an hour had passed, one of the workers shook his head at Ba and Son. "Sorry," he said. "We'll be right back."

Both workers went up the ladder, but the engine still was not fixed. Ba put a pack of cigarettes and a thank-you note in the basket. His note read:

If another boat comes, we can go with them, because our engine is not working.

Soon after the basket went up, it quickly came down with another note.

This is a restricted area. No one is allowed in, so there won't be any boats coming. We are having a meeting and will let you know what we can do for you.

So they waited. Ba puffed on his cigarettes, and everyone else ate some food. Then another note was sent down.

We'll call for help. A boat will come and get you and take you to an island to fix your engine.

Ba had to read the note twice to make sure he understood the words. They were going to be rescued. Some on the little boat hugged each other, while others cheered loudly. As they waited, Ba heard several beeps coming from above and saw a lot of men in orange jumpsuits staring down at them.

"Ba, what's that noise?" asked Quynh.

Ba lifted Quynh onto his lap. "That's Morse code. They're calling out for help. A boat is coming to rescue us."

Quynh and Nhu jumped up and down. "Really? They're coming to save us?" asked Quynh.

Ba smiled and pointed out into the ocean. "Yes. Let me know when you see a boat. You and Nhu. Go tell her to find the boat."

"OK," said Quynh happily. She got off his lap and went to Nhu. Both girls stared out into the ocean, waiting and looking for a boat.

Ba went to Ma, sat next to her, and wrapped an arm around her. Ma sniffled, and Ba wiped away her tears. "Our prayers have been answered," she said.

The workers above began to point out to sea. Quynh and Nhu pointed, too.

"There! See over there!"

A big steel ship came into view with its lights flashing. Workers opened the landing dock, and the vessel stopped moving closer. It was a Chinese naval ship.

Two workers from the oil rig came down the ladder.

"They can't come any closer. Use the oars and row to the ship," said a worker.

Ba and everyone else on the boat bowed their heads and thanked the workers, who, in return, thanked those on the boat and went back up the ladder.

Eight adults grabbed oars and began to row to the naval ship. But as they got closer, the naval ship closed its landing dock and sailed off. On the boat, everyone rowing paused.

Son stood up and lifted a hand to block the sun from his eyes. "Where did they go? Can anyone see it?"

"Should we go back to the rig?" asked Du.

The wind picked up and started to move them in the wrong direction. It was pushing them farther out into the ocean. Ba, Son, Du, and the other men tried to control the boat with the oars, but after fifteen minutes, their efforts proved fruitless. The wind had control of the boat and wasn't going to give it up.

Ba stilled his arms and looked at the others. "Let's all rest awhile."

The others gratefully agreed and put their oars away.

Son looked to where the ship had disappeared. "Where did they go? Did they leave us?"

"Maybe they're testing us," Ba said. "Making sure our engine is really broken?" But he, too, wasn't confident in his answer.

They couldn't go very far rowing, so they just let the wind take them while they rested.

As Ba fished for a cigarette from his pocket, he heard a break in the water and stared at a huge fin. Others also noticed it slowly circling their boat.

"Is that ..." began Son.

"A shark," whispered Du. He tightened his knees to his chest.

Everyone on the boat went silent, staring at the shark fin.

"What should we do?" Son whispered to Ba.

"What can we do? Best to not make any noise and wait for it to leave," said Ba.

Looking back at the oil rig, Ba noticed the lights were flashing in Morse code once more. The workers were calling the naval ship back. They had seen the small children and women and didn't want to leave them out in the ocean with a broken engine.

The shark fin, at last, went back under the water.

"Let's try and row again," said Ba.

Du tightly gripped the oar in his hands. "But what about the shark?"

Ba stuck his oar in the water and gently shook it. "We can use these to attack it. Now, come on. Let's start rowing again."

But it was no use. The wind had taken over and still wasn't ready to let go.

Five minutes later, Son said, "Look."

All turned their heads and saw that the naval ship had returned and was moving toward them. Ma's eyes welled with tears, and Tam gave her a hug. Feelings of relief and excitement filled the boat.

Was this it? Would someone finally come to their rescue? Were they saved?

Along with Ma, many others looked to the sky and thanked the Lord their God for answering their prayers.

As it got closer, the naval ship dropped some rope for Ba and Son to use to tie the fishing boat to the big vessel. A ladder was lowered, and two sailors in uniform climbed down.

"We've come to fix your engine," said one of the sailors. "Please stay here. No one is allowed on the naval ship."

As the men got to work, they turned slightly green. They weren't used to being on a small boat. The waves rocked the men's stomachs. Their heads went over the boat, and both men threw up.

Not being able to take any more, both men climbed back up the ladder. One stopped halfway and looked back down at them. "We'll be right back."

"Please," said Ba. "Please come back. We can't survive without your help."

One of the sailors paused on his way up. He looked down at Ba and glanced at Ma holding Dai Duong. "We'll be back. I give you my word as a father." Up he went and disappeared over the railing, back on the ship.

Ten minutes later, the sailors dropped down a big rope ladder. The sailors motioned for everyone on the boat to climb up. Ba turned to the women and his children. They were in no condition and weren't skilled enough to climb the rope. Ba pointed to the women and children and shook his head. "Please," he called up to the sailors. "The women and children won't be able to climb without help."

Men came down to take the women and children up. One man held Dai Duong in one arm and skillfully climbed up the ladder. Ma got on the back of another sailor. Quynh and Nhu also went up to the ship. Once the women and children were on the backs of sailors and climbing up the rope, Ba turned to the rest of the men. "OK, it's our turn. Climb quickly," he said.

As the men climbed up the rope, some struggled. Du's arms were shaking, and as Son climbed, his foot kept slipping. Their arms were tired from rowing, and the excitement of the day had drained them.

Once all the men had climbed up to the deck, they gathered with the women and girls and collapsed. Ba sat down heavily, gasping for air, and Son lay down on his back with his eyes closed while trying to catch his breath. Ma held Dai Duong close to her chest while Nhu and Quynh sat on either side of her.

Sailors were around them, observing them. One stepped forward. "We're going to tow your boat," he said in Chinese. "But first we have to get the water out."

As the small fishing boat was being towed, two sailors were in it, scooping out buckets of water. Everyone who had been on the fishing boat was tired—tired from a lack of food, tired from the sun's harsh gaze, and tired from rowing. All eighteen of them spread out on the deck and rested.

All but two of the sailors left to resume their duties. The two who stayed kept an eye on the exhausted group.

Curious about what the sailors were doing with the boat, Ba stood on shaking legs and limped his way to the edge of the naval ship. Leaning against a half wall, he looked down. He saw the sailors pouring water out of their boat with buckets. He looked to the distance and wondered where the sailors were taking them.

Ba joined his family and waited for what the sailors would do next.

A half-hour later, three sailors brought them some food.

"Where are you taking us?" asked Ba.

"We're taking you and your family to the nearest island, Hainan Island. A Chinese island." A sailor held out a bowl of rice soup.

Ba took it and bowed his head. "Thank you," he said, raising the dish. "And thank you for taking in my family."

The sailor bowed his head and helped the other sailor pass out the food to the rest of the group. As they distributed rice soup with salt, the sailors couldn't help but stare a second too long at the boat people they'd rescued. Their hair was tangled. Their clothes looked like giant pillowcases on their small bodies. They smelled like dead fish. And their skin was red and blistered.

Nhu and Quynh stuck their noses in the air, sniffing the soup's mouthwatering scent.

"Now, don't eat too fast," said Ba. "Don't want to throw up."

After everyone had eaten as much soup as they could, they all stretched out and tried to get some sleep.

At one o'clock in the morning, the naval ship stopped near Hainan Island. The crew couldn't bring the ship too close because of the rocks surrounding the shore. Rocks were lethal for naval ships; they could puncture the bottom, or the ship could get stuck.

Sailors brought out small boats and lowered them to the water. They would use these to get to the island and tow the fishing boat in to fix the engine.

Ba woke up everyone and gestured for them to follow the sailors. Everyone was divided into three groups to go on three small boats, each no bigger than their fishing boat. Ba and Ma and their girls were together on one boat. Son and his family were on another. And Tam and Du got on the third.

The sailors rowed the boats to the white-sand shore. Once on land, everyone was told to follow the sailors once more. But they had sea legs. No one had touched land for nearly a week. Du walked like he was drunk, fighting against gravity to stay upright. Ba tripped on the sand and felt like his legs were made out of jelly. Ma took her time, calculating every step to make sure she didn't move too quickly. The girls giggled and held on to each other as they tried to stay upright while walking.

Quynh slowed and turned to the ocean, watching their tiny fishing boat being towed to the beach. Ma tugged on her hand, and they caught up with their group.

Ahead sat an old building that looked like some type of warehouse. They stopped before they entered it.

"This is where you'll sleep," said a sailor.

Ba looked around but couldn't see much because of the darkness surrounding them.

Blankets were spread on the porch, and everyone picked a spot to lie down. But all were restless. The shadows outlining the trees and building were unfamiliar to them. For days, all they'd had was the ocean or the moon to help put them to sleep. They hadn't run into trouble with pirates or thieves yet, but what was waiting for them tomorrow? Who was on this island? Would they be accepted on the island? Would they be helped? Or would they be tossed aside and be stuck here—or worse, tossed back into the ocean with a broken boat?

Around him, Ba heard his friends and family tossing and turning nervously. He sat up and cleared his throat. "I know we're all a little scared and not sure what tomorrow brings. But don't worry. Everything will be fine. The naval ship and its sailors rescued us and brought us to this island to fix our boat. They've fed us and given us a place to sleep. I want you all to try to not worry. Get the rest we all need and put your worries aside for tomorrow."

Ba's girls told him good night, and Son thanked him for his words. Some were reassured by Ba's speech and were able to rest. It calmed the nerves of others, who were able to fall asleep while looking at the stars.

Ma peeked at Nhu and saw her fussing. She wiped the sweat from her forehead. "Sleep, my daughter. Sleep, close your eyes, and dream," cooed Ma.

Ma twirled Nhu's hair until the child closed her eyes and went to sleep. Ma let her go and tucked the blanket around Dai Duong. She kissed her forehead and closed her own eyes.

The Island

July 6, 1979

W hen the sun rose and colored the earth, everyone was wakened by an officer from the island. He studied the group, his dark-brown eyes scrutinizing all of them.

"How many of you are here?" he asked curtly.

"Eighteen, including the baby," said Ba.

The officer paced slowly in front of them and stopped. "Do any of you have watches? Gold?" Nodding toward the other sailors, he said, "Have them turn out their pockets."

Everyone had hardly anything. Just the clothes on their backs.

Tam, with shaky hands, took a ring off her finger. She stared at it until a sailor snatched it. Another woman, a relative of Son's, was biting her lip and twisting a ring around her finger. The sailor went to her and held out his hand, waiting. The woman, with tears in her eyes, slipped off the ring and handed it to the sailor.

All the jewelry that the sailors collected totaled an ounce of gold. Ba hid his watch, knowing that if he gave it up, he would lose track of time and day when they got back out to sea.

Back at the shore, sailors had hauled the fishing boat farther onto the sand and towed it to a truck. They took the boat to a mechanic shop and tore the engine apart.

After the sailors had collected all the gold from the group of eighteen, they escorted everyone to a beach bonfire, where men cooked rice and fish. Each person was handed some food, and they spread out along the sand to eat.

Ba and the others took a look around the beach. The sand beneath their feet was white and bounced when they walked. Palm trees lined up along the beach as if they were protecting the island. A gentle breeze made the leaves dance and wave. Surrounding some of the palm trees were white orchids dancing along with the leaves of the palm trees. On the beach were fallen coconuts and a small dock, where there were small fishing boats for the locals.

At the docks, men were preparing their boats, gathering up their fishing poles and nets for their catches.

When Ba and Son finished their food, they were taken to the mechanic shop.

Meanwhile, at the beach, Quynh and Nhu played with the water, chasing it down as the ocean ebbed and running back up the shore as the water chased after them. Ma—sitting under the shade of a palm tree while nursing Dai Duong—watched over the girls.

At the mechanic shop, Ba and Son saw the boat and the engine torn apart.

A sailor walked up to them. "I have a few things to show you. But before I do, I want to tell you what to do since you have water in your boat: you need to flip the boat over to get the water out."

Five sailors, with the help of Ba and Son, went around the boat and did exactly that. Water splashed onto the dirt floor, some drops hitting Ba's and Son's feet.

The sailor held out some wood siding. "We use this to help fill in the gaps. And we have the usual glue to patch up the wood. This will help stop the water from leaking in."

Then the sailor handed Ba some tar-like material and showed him how to use it on the boat. "You see all these gaps? Use this to fill them in."

Ba happily took the tools and got to work. He would do anything to get this boat ready so that they could continue their trip to Hong Kong.

Son also grabbed some, and the men worked on the boat, filling all the gaps.

When that was finished, they waited for the glue to dry, and the sailor brought in the next thing to do.

"Now we paint over the boat. This is a protective layer for the wood. We use this so the wood won't be ruined by the salt water."

As the men worked on the boat, Ba patted the side of it, hoping that the engine could be fixed. They were so close to their final destination. Their boat had gotten them this far—it just had to stay together a little longer.

Ma and the rest of the group were back at the warehouse's porch. Sailors came and gave them extra firewood, as well as pots and pans to borrow, and salt and oil for cooking over the beach bonfire. The travelers weren't sure how long they would have to stay on the island until their boat was fixed. Until then, the local people also helped them out.

Those who lived on the island were poor fisherman, government employees, and oil-rig workers. They would grab their nets and wade out into the water, spears in hand. Others went on their fishing boats and headed out to the ocean to catch as much fish as they could.

Along the shores were coconut trees. Young and able men were climbing up the trees and collecting as many coconuts as they could, dropping them down on the sand.

Quynh and Nhu went to inspect one of the coconuts. A man jumped down from the tree and showed the girls how to get food out of it. He used a machete to open the coconut. He handed one half to Quynh and the other to Nhu.

"Thank you," the girls said, then they giggled and ran to their mother.

"What do you have there?" Ma asked as she rocked Dai Duong.

"A coconut," said Nhu.

They all gathered together to eat some coconut and drink its sweet juice.

Midafternoon, one of the men fixing the boat handed Ba and Son a bucket each.

"Always starting at three o'clock, the boats come back in. Go to the docks and ask for some fish," said the man.

Ba and Son thanked the man, took their buckets, and headed to the docks. The man was right. At the docks, fishing boats were coming back from the ocean. The men on the boats were smiling at one another and talking about their biggest catch. Some with their collected fish, would sell them to the markets in town. Ba and Son stood at the docks and thanked every fisherman who scooped some fish into their buckets. Son and Ba went back to their people with two full buckets. For dinner, they cooked fish and drank coconut juice. The children and adults alike were given the same rations of food.

After enjoying a big meal and with full stomachs, everyone gathered around the firepit—people cuddling up to their families and watching the flames dance with the wind. Red, orange, and yellow colors swam like mermaid tails.

The fishermen on the island were generous with their fish, knowing that the eighteen people gathered together were hungry. Ma and the others were very thankful for the fishermen who thought of them and gave them food. All felt supported and knew that they were in good hands until their boat was fixed. They even made friends with some of the fishermen.

They had been on the island now for several days. To pass the time while the boat was getting fixed, Du and others would go with the fishermen on their boats to help catch fish and learn a few tricks on how to catch them.

One day, a fisherman made the group pork with a lot of fat in it. Everyone moaned while they ate it and, when they were done, licked their lips. But the next day, their stomachs were in agony. Their insides seemed to twist and turn, and no one could escape what was coming: diarrhea.

From then on, they stuck to fresh fish and rice cooked by Tam and Ma. Sometimes, they were able to add salt and chili peppers to their meals for extra flavor.

The island was filled with flies and mosquitoes. Flies were everywhere, buzzing above people's heads and hovering around the food. At night, mosquitoes came out and tried to suck up as much blood as they could. Slaps were heard throughout the night as people tried to wave away the bugs or kill them on their arms and legs.

Also, those on the island had told the newcomers to be careful when walking beneath the coconut trees. You could easily die if a coconut fell off a tree and struck you on the head. The locals also warned them about venturing to the south side. There was no beach there—just giant rocks and a cliff. Some of the local men would go there to dive from the rocks, but they had to be careful not to slip on them. They didn't want to hit their head, get knocked out, and drown in the ocean.

During the day, the children would play in the ocean. They didn't go too deep because they didn't know how to swim. They went in just far enough to splash one another. Seeing the kids playing made some of the adults join them. They relaxed in the water, trying to cool off from the unforgiving heat.

To pass the time on the island, the girls played *choi chuyen*, also known as bamboo jacks. They taught the local fisherman how to play. One day, Quynh found ten sticks, and Nhu got a rock. The objective of the game was to toss a rock into the air and pick up as many sticks as possible before trying to catch the rock before it landed—all while singing a song.

Quynh took the rock from Nhu, tossed it in the air, and began to sing, *"Cai mot, cai mai, cai co, so mang, thang chang, con chit, ngam nga, ngam nguyt, chuot chit, sang ban doi."*

She picked up six sticks and caught the rock. She handed the rock to a local fisherman. "Now you try," she said. "Nhu and I will sing for you."

The man spoke to them in Chinese, and the girls giggled. The girls sang as the fisherman tossed the rock in the air, picked up three sticks, fumbled with the rock, and ended up dropping everything. The girls rolled on their backs and laughed.

Ma smiled, hearing her girls' laughter. Her heart lightened at the sight and the sound of them being able to be kids again. In her arms was Dai Duong, sleeping.

Ma looked toward a path that led away from the beach toward the mechanic shop. She heard hammers beating down on metal and a saw cutting wood. She didn't know how long they would have to stay on the island until their boat was fixed. But she knew all about patience and about her faith in God when it came to waiting. Ma knew too well the fear of doubt in her mind and at the bottom of her stomach. She had experienced this feeling before, specifically while waiting to hear from Ba when the communists had won. She remembered thinking every morning when she woke up, *Will this be the day they send me a letter of my husband's death? Will this be the day that I finally hear from him?*

After Ma's parents left for America, Ma took the girls to her aunt's house for a while and then moved in permanently with Ba's family. There were whispers of reeducation camps that seemed to have sprouted in the night. At first, all that was said about these camps was that soldiers and others against communism were sent to them to be reeducated on the new government and to leave all their old views behind. But then weeks passed and there was different talk about these reeducation camps and how they weren't even camps at all. They were prison camps where men were tortured, abused, and starved.

Ma would kneel in front of her bed, squeeze her hands tight, bow her head, and pray to God. She'd ask Him where her husband was. Had he been taken to those camps that she heard about? Or could he be somewhere worse? Was he lost out in the wild? Was he dead, his body yet to be discovered?

Ma felt tears come to her eyes as she remembered those dark days and the dark thoughts that plagued her mind. It had been hard going to sleep at night when half the bed was empty. It had been hard to watch her girls play, grow, and learn, knowing that their father wasn't there to experience it with her. She'd ask herself, *Will Phu miss this?*

Twice a day, Quynh and Nhu would ask her where Ba was—and Ma would always repeat the same answer: "He'll be home soon." She dreaded the day when the girls would stop asking.

One day, a motorcycle stopped in front of their house. When she heard it outside, Ma, who was in the kitchen, set down a damp towel that she had used just seconds before to wipe her hands. The kitchen walls were painted banana yellow, and the floor was made of wooden planks. Lying atop the four-seat table was a freshly cleaned white cloth. The table was set with white porcelain plates, bowls, and cups decorated with flowers drawn in light-blue ink. Plants were hanging from the ceiling, and a big pot in the corner contained a tall plant reaching for the ceiling.

Ma inched her way to the door in the living room. This room was painted white and had the same wooden-plank floor. The furniture, all made with wood, featured green cushions. On a side table was a golden Buddha. Three wooden shelves on the walls held picture frames, a jade-green clock, and candles that smelled of pomelo. Scattered across the coffee table were dolls and clothing that belonged to the girls.

There was a knock coming from the front door. Ma opened the door gingerly.

A man bowed his head to her. "Family Nguyen?"

"Yes," she said.

He handed her a letter. "For you."

Ma took the letter and bowed her head. "Thank you."

He returned the bow and got back on his motorcycle. Ma closed the door and leaned against it.

Coming from a bedroom were squeals of delight as Quynh and Nhu were playing and causing mischief.

Ma stared at the worn envelope, which was faded and, at one corner, bent. With trembling fingers, she slid her finger under the envelope and hissed in pain. A paper cut.

She stuck her finger in her mouth to stop the bleeding and resumed opening the envelope. Her eyes were having trouble concentrating. It took her a while to read it because her eyes jumped ahead on the page and she constantly had to go back and reread.

Once she finished reading the letter, she sat down heavily on the floor and dropped the letter. Her mother-in-law came from the bathroom, wiping her damp hands on her dress.

"What is it, Nga? Is it from Phu?" Bà Nội bent down and picked up the letter. It was a letter from her son, in his own handwriting, stating that he was still alive and being held captive in a reeducation camp.

As she read, tears came to her eyes and she put a hand on her mouth.

When she finished, she helped Ma off the floor and embraced her, stroking her hair. "It's all right now. We found him. He's still alive."

For a moment, Ma felt at peace. Her husband was alive. The months of waiting and not escaping with her family had been worth it. But then a sense of dread crept back into the bottom of Ma's stomach. Ba, for all those months, had been in those prison camps. She could not bear the thought of what her husband had to endure and for how long. Now she had to figure out if there was a way she could see him and get him out.

Ma hastily wiped away her tears as the girls came running to her from the beach.

"Ma, we made a new friend," said Quynh.

"We played choi chuyen," said Nhu.

"Did you girls win?" asked Ma.

The girls giggled and nodded.

"What's all this giggling?" said a voice.

The girls turned to their father and ran toward him, telling him about their new friend and how they won playing choi chuyen. Ba widened his eyes and gasped when the girls told their story, and Ma laughed. Right now, her heart couldn't be more content than when she received that letter four years earlier announcing that Ba was still alive. All that worry about Ba's missing out on his girls was washed away, like the ocean water flowing away from the shore. Here he was today, able to create a memory with them—and many more in the future.

Leaving the Island

July 17, 1979

A voice yelled, "Phu, Phu, the boat. It's fixed."

Ba finished eating and turned around to see Son running to the beach. Behind him were five sailors towing the fishing boat back to the shore.

Son was smiling ear to ear and stopped next to Ba. "They want the boat to be tested."

Ba stood. "I'll do it."

"Is it truly fixed?" asked Ma.

"We're about to find out," said Ba. He kissed the top of her head and followed the boat.

"Be careful," she said.

"Where's Ba going?" asked Quynh.

"He's going to take the boat out and see if the engine works," said Ma.

"I don't want to go back on the boat," said Quynh.

"Yeah, me neither," said Nhu.

Ma gently stroked her daughters' hair. "I know you don't. But we can't stay on this island forever. Remember, we're supposed to go to Hong Kong. And then America, where my parents and siblings are waiting for us."

The girls watched the sailors as they untied the boat and pushed it into the water. Five sailors from the island went with Ba on the boat, and he started the engine. He grinned and patted it. "Come on, don't fail me now."

"When the boat is fixed, we won't be at sea for very long this time," said Ma.

"Promise?" asked Quynh.

Ma gave her a smile. "I promise."

Back on the boat, Ba and the sailors drove around. Ba twisted and turned the boat, testing the engine. While he was turning, something big emerged from the depths of the ocean.

Another man on the boat stood and shouted, "Submarine!"

All the men on the boat watched the submarine emerge. As time passed, it went back down.

"Do you see them very often?" Ba asked a man.

He nodded. "Not very. But we see them from time to time."

After twenty minutes, the engine sputtered and, with a last bang, died. They had gone out only a couple of miles to test it. The boat stopped, and all the men looked at the engine with their mouths wide open.

A sailor cleared his throat and grabbed an oar. "Well, better it breaks down now than when you take it out there with your family." He held out an oar to Ba, who stared at it.

He couldn't believe it. The engine had once again failed. Ba sighed deeply and took the oar.

All six had to row back to the beach. Back at shore, they pushed the boat to land and towed it inland once more to the mechanic shop.

Son went to Ba. "What happened? Why is it being towed back?"

Ba sighed. "Water got in the engine. They're going to work on it again." He shook his head and threw the oar onto the sand. "That damn boat just keeps letting us down."

Son squeezed Ba's shoulder. "It'll be all right, Phu. We have all the time in the world to get it fixed, fixed to get us safely to Hong Kong. Glad it broke down now rather than out in the ocean again."

The next day, Ma and Tam had taken Quynh and Nhu to the beach. Tam picked up a sand dollar and showed it to the girls. "Let's collect some seashells."

Quynh and Nhu ran along the beach collecting shells. They collected tiny pearl-white ones that swirled. They collected light-pink seashells, as well as ones with brown spots.

Ma smiled at her girls, rocking a sleeping Dai Duong.

"It's good to see them have fun," said Tam. "And not just them. Everyone else, too. Being out on the ocean was rough."

"This island is a blessing," said Ma. "God knew we needed help and got us here."

When they got back to their camping spot on the beach, Nhu and Quynh went to Ba and showed him their collection.

"Wow," he said. "Look at all those shells you collected."

"Here, Ba," said Quynh. She handed him a black seashell. "I got this one for you."

Nhu handed Ba a faded-yellow seashell that was spiky.

"Thank you, daughters," said Ba. He put them in his pocket and patted it. "I'll keep them safe and cherish them forever."

Later that day, the group's twelfth on the island, Ba went to the sailors' office and noticed hanging on the wall behind the officer's desk a big map of the world.

"Hello, Phu. What can I do for you?" asked the officer in charge. He saw Ba staring at the map.

"When our engine is fixed, we'll set out again for Hong Kong. May I have the map to help us get there?" asked Ba.

89

"No," said the officer. "But here, I have some paper and pencil for you to trace the map." He grabbed them and handed them to Ba. Ba bowed his head, went to the map, and traced it.

"Could you go along China's shorelines with us, in case something goes wrong with our boat?" asked Ba.

"Unfortunately, we cannot. There are rocks there that can destroy our naval ship," said the officer. He went next to Ba and pointed at the map. "You need to go ninety degrees for six to seven hours, then turn at fifty to fifty-five degrees here. Be careful of the rocks, they could sink your boat. So make sure you're deep out in the water, so you hit nothing." The officer stepped back and sat back down. "It would be best if you leave in the afternoon—the water is calmer, and there will be less waves."

"Thank you," Ba said. "And I was wondering how it was coming along with our boat?"

The officer collected some papers and straightened them on his desk. "It should be done today. If you wanted, you could leave first thing tomorrow afternoon."

Ba thanked the officer again and made his way back to his group. He updated everyone on his conversation with the officer.

"So, we'll leave tomorrow?" asked Du.

"Yes," said Ba. "We leave tomorrow in the afternoon. We have some time to gather supplies for hopefully our last trip across the ocean on that boat."

In preparation for their trip to Hong Kong, the locals gave them supplies. They provided crackers, as well as eight clay containers filled with water and covered with banana leaves to prevent spilling. They also included two cans of diesel; some Chinese medicine for stomachaches and headaches; a hurricane lantern; and coconuts and fish.

Later that afternoon, Ba, Son, and some of the local sailors took the boat out again in the ocean to test it. When minutes had passed and the engine continued chugging along, Ba and Son shared a smile. They brought their boat to the docks, and Ba told everyone the great news.

"We'll be leaving tomorrow, for sure. This will be our last night on the island."

Everyone sighed in relief. Some, including Ma, raised their hands in the air and thanked God for answering their prayers.

The next day, they left at three o'clock in the afternoon. The fishermen helped refresh their memory on which way to go in the ocean and told them to avoid a particular route because the water was unstable and dangerous. They showed Ba the best way to get to Hong Kong.

The group of eighteen had spent thirteen days on the island. They thanked the fishermen for all their help during their stay Ma bowed her head briefly and thanked God for the welcome detour. She felt she and the seventeen others were lucky to have come across such gracious people. She prayed for them and wished them well.

"Be careful," said one fisherman. "Not all fishermen are true out there. Some followed the path of crime and became pirates themselves."

"Thank you," said Son. "We'll look out for any boats we see out there."

The fishermen wished them all a safe journey to Hong Kong, and the refugees were back on the boat and about to be on their way.

As they pushed off from the docks and headed to the ocean, the local fishermen gathered around and sang the song the girls had taught them when they were playing choi chuyen: "*Cai mot, cai mai, cai co, so mang, thang chang, con chit, ngam nga, ngam nguyt, chuot chit, sang ban doi.*"

The girls waved toward shore until the island disappeared.

Ba took charge of driving the boat. He patted the engine, hoping that this time it wouldn't break down. They were so close to their destination. The engine had to hang on just a little longer. One day. That's all they had left to get to Hong Kong.

For the first hour, they traveled without incident. Their engine continued pushing them forward and the ocean was still.

Du put his hands on his lap and tightened his body. He kept glancing at the engine, waiting for it to break down. He made himself look away from it and prayed instead. His eyes stared at the sea that had turned black as a witch's brew. He closed his eyes, not wanting to look at anything. His throat tightened and his nose began to sting. Tears fell down his cheeks. He held his head in his hands so no one could see.

What if this is it? Du wondered. *What if the engine dies again and this time, no one comes to help? Will we die along with the engine?*

At four o'clock, it began to rain. Lightning flashed across the sky and thunder rumbled above them. Rain poured down on them like a cold shower. Nhu and Quynh went down below, hugging each other. Fish began jumping out of the water and getting into the boat.

"Hurry," Ba shouted over the rain. "Get the fish out."

Everyone's hands—slippery with rainwater and fish slime—tried to toss the fish from the boat. The fish were coming onto the boat as fast as they were being thrown out. Ba was afraid that their boat would sink due to the heavy weight of the fish. The fish that came flying out of the water slapped people across their cheeks and the backs of their heads. People dodged and swatted at the fish as they came jumping in.

Ma went down below with the girls and leaned over a crying Dai Duong, trying to keep her as dry as possible and make sure no fish hurt her.

When the rain finally settled, no more fish jumped into their boat. Ba and Son sat down with a relieved sigh.

"Ma, are we there yet?" asked Quynh. "Why is it taking so long?"

Ma stroked Quynh's hair. "We'll be there soon."

"How soon? I thought we'd be there by now," said Quynh.

"We all did. But the engine broke down and we had to get it fixed. It shouldn't be long now."

Before nightfall, Du had his hands on his stomach once more, familiar with the swirling. He wasn't the only one seasick. Others had hands on their bellies or mouths. Some couldn't hold it in and puked over the side.

Du had had enough. He was sick of this boat, sick of the overly happy bright sky, and sick of the stretch of endless sea blue. He was sick of feeling sick.

He hated how closely everyone was compacted in this tiny boat. He wanted his own space. Wanted to stretch out his limbs and get comfortable. Comfortable seemed foreign to him. He missed eating food that wasn't soaked with ocean water, he missed sleeping on a comfortable bed, he missed the wind of a fan to cool him off, and he missed the comfort of a fire when he woke up shivering in the middle of the night.

He hated the sun's heat. It burned, turning everyone's skin red. Some did whatever they could for shade: shielded themselves with their arms, went under the wooden planks, or put clothes or bags over their heads.

Du despised lying under the boat's planks. He felt trapped and couldn't breathe fresh air. If it was even possible, it seemed to be hotter underneath than it was sitting above.

When it finally got dark, Du was able to relax. The heat wasn't as blazing, and if they got lucky, a cool breeze would provide them some comfort.

At nine o'clock, Ba stood and saw ahead in the distance some lights and fishing boats. Ba and the others gasped at the tall buildings in the distance.

At last, they had made it to the bay of Hong Kong.

"Hurry, Phu," said someone.

"Go faster," said someone else.

"No. We have to go slow. We don't want to hit any rocks. Son, get out the big stick," said Ba.

Son got the big stick and went to the front of the boat. He occasionally poked the stick into the water, checking for rocks beneath. And if their boat got too close to rocks, Son used the stick to push the boat away. But with night having closed in, Ba couldn't see what lay ahead, and Son couldn't tell if there were rocks nearby.

"We'll stop here for the night," said Ba. "Don't want to risk the rocks hitting us, not when we're so close." He turned off the engine. "We wait for daylight."

Son put the big stick away and went back to Ba. "We'll take turns on watch. Make sure we don't go farther in or go back," said Ba.

Hong Kong

July 20, 1979

A t sunrise, a boat engine woke up almost everyone. The children were sleeping soundly.

Ba and Son looked and saw a police boat heading their way. The sirens turned on, and the children sat up, wide-eyed and bewildered.

"It's OK," said Ma. Her girls were curled on either side of her, and Dai Duong was on her lap. "It's all right. Just a police boat."

The police boat pulled up next to the little fishing boat. An officer bowed his head and asked in English, "Who is the captain?"

Ba turned to Son and said, "You better speak to them. Your English is better than mine."

Son turned to the policeman and nodded. "I'm the captain."

"How many of you are there?" asked the officer.

"Eighteen, including the baby," Son said, pointing to Dai Duong.

"Stay right there," said the officer. He went to his radio control and sent out a message in Morse code.

Thirty minutes passed, then everyone heard a noise coming from the sky. All eyes looked up and saw a helicopter coming their way. It hovered right above their fishing boat. Inside were two White Englishmen and an interpreter from Hong Kong. One of the Englishmen was holding a camera and aiming it down at their little fishing boat. He also had a video camera nearby.

The helicopter stirred up heavy waves, rocking the boat violently. Dai Duong started to cry and everyone held on to the boat. Water splashed in, and Ba grabbed the big stick to motion in the air for the helicopter to fly up higher. The helicopter rose higher—and the waves subsided. The boat returned to lying still on the water.

The police officer motioned for Son to get on his boat to answer more questions.

"Where have you all come from?" asked the officer.

"Vietnam. Our engine died on the way here. While our engine was dead in the water, we made do with making a sail out of a blanket. One of the women on the boat gave birth. We finally came upon an oil rig, and they called a naval ship to help us out. We were stuck on Hainan Island for days, waiting for our boat to get fixed. We just left yesterday from the island and got here late last night. Didn't want to risk destroying our boat from rocks, so we waited until there was light," said Son. He glanced up at the helicopter. "What are they doing here?"

"That's BBC News," said the officer, referring to the British Broadcasting Company. "They must have heard us talk about your boat on the radio. They came here to do a documentary on refugee boat people."

From the helicopter, a ladder was dropped down, and the two Englishmen—a cameraman and an interviewer, both in their thirties—came down the ladder and got on the boat.

Ba went to them and bowed his head. "Please," he began. "I'm worried about all the weight on the boat."

The cameraman hopped onto the police boat and the interviewer stayed on the fishing boat. "Does anyone speak English or French?" he asked.

Ba nodded, saying in broken English, "A little of both."

While the interviewer talked to Ba in English, the cameraman took pictures of their boat, his camera clicking and flashing. He took pictures of all eighteen people crammed on the boat and zoomed in on Ma holding Dai Duong.

The interviewer then began asking questions and writing on a pad of paper.

"Where did you all come from? How long did it take you to get here? I'd like to know more about the baby. Was she born before or on the boat?"

When he finished asking questions and heard their story, he joined the cameraman on the police boat. Both Englishmen went to the police officer.

"We're doing a story on boat people. Heard on the radio about this fishing boat with some children and a baby," said the interviewer. "We're doing an hour documentary about boat refugees." He turned to Son and said, "Would you mind taking the boat back out in the ocean, so we can get some video footage of you arriving here?"

"Hang on," said Son. He went back to the fishing boat and told Ba everything he heard and explained the interviewer's request.

Ba sighed heavily. "Son, we're all tired. We're so close to the shore. Let's just go there."

A Red Cross boat and a fire department boat pulled up alongside the police boat.

"It'll be fine," said Son. "It won't take too long. And it's not every day we have a camera crew with us."

Ba reluctantly agreed and took the boat back into the ocean. The police boat, with the BBC News crew on it, wasn't too far behind.

It took two hours to record them going back in.

As they headed toward shore—with the helicopter above them and the police boat not too far behind—they passed lots of fishing boats going toward the ocean with their fishing poles and nets, as well as boats motoring back in with their daily catch.

On their own boat, Ba heard voices rise in excitement. They could see buildings, tall and growing, reaching for the clouds. A bigger Red Cross boat sailed up next to theirs. Some men on it waved their arms, and Ba stopped the boat.

"Come aboard," said a man. "We'll tow your boat the rest of the way."

Ba and the others collected what they had left and boarded the Red Cross boat.

Ba carried Nhu and tightly gripped the railing as he got on the Red Cross boat. Ma held Dai Duong close to her chest as she waited for Ba and Nhu. Once Ba set down Nhu, he held out his hand to Ma and helped her across. Next, Tam jumped across like a graceful deer. Du carried Quynh and stumbled when he jumped across. Tam and Ba helped him regain his balance. Everyone else grabbed the railing, reached for Ba's hand, or jumped across. Before the group had even settled in, the men on the Red Cross boat tied the fishing boat behind their boat and headed toward shore.

Two men came forward, one holding a hose that was attached to a bottle of disinfectant.

"We must clean you before you enter the camp," said a man.

Everyone spread out, and they were sprayed with white powder. Another man had come forward to hold Dai Duong while Ma got sprayed.

Up in the sky, the helicopter recorded everything—its blades going *womp, womp, womp.*

A Red Cross man handed Ba a piece of paper with the number 845.

Ba stared at it. *Is that how many boats have come to* just *Hong Kong?* he wondered. Eight hundred and forty-five boats, coming from Vietnam to Hong Kong. Escaping a country that no longer cared for its citizens. Eight hundred and forty-four other boats had already escaped to get there. Who knew how many more boats were out there, on their way or heading to other countries.

Ba looked back at the ocean. *Is there a number for how many boats didn't make it?* he thought. He glanced up at the helicopter and the cameras all around them, videotaping and taking pictures. This was all surreal, because for weeks they had been just trying to survive and escape. There they were now, with every move they made captured on film. It was a lot for Ba to process.

They passed other boats, some bigger and others smaller than their own. All were just as packed as theirs, with people piled on top of people. Ba had trouble not staring at one boat in particular. It was carrying only one woman and three children.

When Ba's group made it to the dock, there were several thousand people all gathered around.

"This is the immigration dock with a refugee camp nearby," said the Red Cross captain. "Already holding ten thousand refugees."

"Ten thousand?" whispered Ba.

Ten thousand people—families, parents, grandparents, children, and friends—had left behind their homes and possessions. All in search of a better life. Of a future.

"Each of you will be processed here. Your pictures will be taken, and you'll be interviewed," said the captain. "Welcome to Black Camp."

Refugee Camp, Hong Kong. Photo courtesy of BBC News.

When they got to the dock, everyone got off the Red Cross boat, and their fishing boat was tied to the dock. Getting used to walking on land took them a while. They tripped on their own feet, and it took them twice as long to get to the line to enter camp because they were stumbling.

The BBC News crew followed them to the line and recorded their movements and those of the other families in line. Ba was intrigued by the news crew documenting their journey. The crew would accompany them every step of the way.

Ma patted Dai Duong as she looked over the line of other families. She wondered what their life stories were and how they had gotten there. Had they all been packed on small boats, or did they get bigger boats? Did any of them run into pirates? Master the storms? Pass other boats across the sea? Overcome dehydration and starvation?

Du stretched his legs and broke out into a big smile. They had finally made it, finally gotten to Hong Kong. He glanced back at the ocean and shivered. Never again.

There was a long line of people entering the camp. Families stood or sat together. Umbrellas were opened to block the sun, while some people found cardboard and held it over their heads.

Waiting in line, they walked around or jumped in place as they tried to get their land legs back.

By late afternoon, Ba and the others were at the front of the line. Du stared at the gate entrance and the high walls surrounding the camp. At the top of the walls was barbed wire. And people at the gate had weapons. Ba and the rest were taken to a room with a big table and enough chairs for all eighteen to sit together. The news crew entered and gave them some pop and cookies to enjoy while waiting to be interviewed by immigration officials.

Quynh and Nhu sipped the pop and giggled.

"It bubbles in your mouth," said Quynh.

They enjoyed their cookies, gobbling up the chocolate chips and rubbing their bellies. The girls had missed the taste of sugar.

Above the door was a No Smoking sign, but Ba ignored it or, in his nervous state, didn't see it. He took out a cigarette and smoked it to provide himself with comfort and satisfy his craving.

If a policeman caught someone smoking, they would hit them and treat them like a criminal. This rule was put in place because the policemen and people running the camp were afraid of starting a fire. The quarters were already tight, given the thousands of refugees there, so a fire would easily engulf everything and everyone.

Ba and Ma's group felt privileged because of the news crew following them around, curious about their story and how they had arrived with a newborn baby and other children.

Each person in their group was interviewed and asked for their date of birth and where they were from. Then each had to be checked by the doctors and nurses to make sure they were in good health.

After being processed, Ba wrapped an arm around Ma and gave her a gentle squeeze. They did it. After nineteen long, grueling days, they were finally in Hong Kong.

Ma buried her head against Ba's neck. "You did this, Phu. You did all of this to bring our family here. None of us would be here without you."

"We all did this. We all did our part to get here," said Ba.

"But it all started because of you. I thank God every day for bringing you into my life. We have three beautiful girls and are so close to starting over."

"We're close. We still just have to take it one day at a time," said Ba.

By afternoon, Ba and Ma were done being interviewed by immigration officials. They left the building and were being watched by policemen.

The eighteen-person group had been broken down into two groups: Ba, Ma, Quynh, Nhu, Dai Duong, Du, and Tam were together, while Son and his family were assigned to a different area of the camp.

"We'll take you to a place where you can stay for a while," a police officer told Ba.

Ba and his family went deeper into Black Camp and headed to an old warehouse in the distance. Their group huddled together as they walked through tents and different buildings. People stared at them as they walked by. The smells of body odor and grilled food filled the air. Due to the number of people, refugees were lucky if they were able to take a shower or bath. Water ran out quickly, and the lines were spread out like ants entering an ant hill.

They passed a play area with a wooden boat that had been towed in for the kids. Sand was spread around. A couple of guards were trying to teach some of the kids how to play catch with an empty can.

On the way to the warehouse, the group passed people who had gathered in a circle to show or do artwork. Artists had canvases and paper spread out on the ground, along with pencils, charcoal, paint, and other tools they were using to create masterpieces.

Quynh and Nhu pointed at the paintings and drawings. "Pretty," they said.

"Ma, can we draw, too?" asked Quynh.

Ma pulled Quynh's hand gently to catch up with their group. "Maybe later. Come on now."

Inside the warehouse were bright lights. The group passed other families, each of which had been given a section of floor, as well as blankets and sleeping mats. The warehouse was as packed as a busy supermarket. People and their children sat on bunk beds or blankets spread across the floor. Above them were clothes hanging to dry out. Spread around the warehouse were metal buckets to catch the water leaking through the roof. Because of the number of boat people arriving every day, camp workers set up tents and spread them out. As more boat people came in, more toilets either broke or were used more. There weren't enough toilets, so some people were forced to use the bushes and leaves.

A police officer stopped in front of a large open space on the floor. He went to a locked storage area and took out some blankets and sleeping mats. He handed them to Ba, and the group spread out the blankets and mats on the floor.

Their space was big enough to fit all seven of them. It wasn't too crowded; they all fit good enough.

The cameraman had his left eye squeezed shut as he recorded them settling into their space on the floor.

"Down the hall is where you all share the toilets. We'll be back to give you some food," said the police officer loudly over the noise of children playing and crying.

Ba and Ma looked around at other families huddled together on the floor.

"How long do you think we'll have to stay here?" asked Ma.

Ba shrugged his shoulders. "I'm not sure. Long enough for them to clear our paperwork."

"And then what?" asked Quynh.

"Then we go home," said Ba.

"Vietnam or America?" asked Quynh.

"America, silly. Remember, we're going to have a new home in America," said Ba.

A police officer later came back with dinner and handed out milk cans, canned foods, slices of bread, oranges, and apples. Ba and Ma gathered their girls and handed out the food. The girls ate as much as they could. Ba enjoyed every bite, and Ma was grateful that her family was there eating food and no longer drifting on the ocean. Du and Tam ate, too, and enjoyed each other's company.

At eight o'clock that night, the policemen came back for a roll call to make sure everyone was there and where they were supposed to be in the warehouse.

Ba lay down next to Ma, their three girls between them. The girls were peacefully asleep. Ma closed her eyes and wrapped an arm around Dai Duong.

Ba was the last to close his eyes. Despite the thousands of refugees asleep all around him, he wasn't bothered. Ba and Ma and the others had done the impossible and had made it to Hong Kong. Now there was nothing else to do but wait for their paperwork.

Telegram

July 21, 1979

E arly one morning, a voice called out, "Breakfast! Wake up for breakfast."

The girls were the first up. Quynh shook Ba's shoulder while Nhu copied her and shook Ma's shoulder.

"Breakfast. Get up. I'm hungry," said Quynh.

Ba sat up and stretched. It had been a while since he had been able to sleep through the night.

Policemen were handing out food to families, and they gave Ba, Ma, and the others some bread, more cans of milk, and more fruit.

As they settled on the floor, the BBC News crew came in, set up their cameras, and pointed them at the group. The crew watched as the family ate their breakfast.

Ma chewed on her apple slice thoughtfully and glanced at the crew. She wondered if they could help her get a message to her family in America.

Ma handed Dai Duong over to Tam and went to the cameraman. "Excuse me," she said in broken English.

The cameraman smiled down at her. "Is there something I can help you with?"

"Telegram. To America. To parents," said Ma.

Ma's parents and seven siblings had fled Vietnam four years earlier and safely settled in America. She thought back to that heart-wrenching day when she first tried to escape with them. She wanted to get word to them that she made it to Hong Kong.

After Ma's parents—Ông Ngoại and Bà Ngoại—dropped her off back in Vietnam, they sailed for five days before arriving at St. John's Island in Singapore.

Most of their journey was in sunshine. Rain didn't come down hard on them, and wind didn't blow them over. They didn't run into pirates and experienced no danger. Their boat journey was smooth sailing.

On the island in Singapore, they stayed at an ex-military base camp. The beaches were covered in warm yellow sand, and the ocean water rushed up in tones of blue, teal, and green. The trees were tall and lushly green. The island was blooming in colors of strawberry pink, bumblebee yellow, cantaloupe orange, galaxy purple, butterfly blue, and poppy red.

Ma's parents and siblings stayed there with other refugees for four months, waiting for resettlement. Refugees worked to find sponsors from churches in France and the United States.

The Church of Jesus Christ of Latter-day Saints in Springfield, Missouri, helped sponsor Bà Ngoại and her family. Eventually, they helped bring them to America.

Glenn Yoeman was the minister of the Mormon church. The same church had sponsored other relatives months earlier.

Bà Ngoại and her family lived together in a four-bedroom apartment that the church helped pay for until the family had some money coming in from their jobs. A total of nine people lived there: Bà Ngoại, Ông Ngoại, and their seven children. All seven kids were enrolled in school while the adults had jobs. Di Nguyet, Bà Ngoại's daughter, enrolled in Drury College at age eighteen. Other family members, with help from the church, were able to get jobs at a Chinese restaurant called Mr. Egg Roll. They worked at the restaurant after school.

Ông Ngoại got a job as a mechanic and helped build alternators. He had never worked around cars in Vietnam. He felt like a servant because there was a lot of work to be done. But he never complained.

Bà Ngoại eventually got a job at the Sisters of Visitation, a convent, where she worked as a cook.

After several years of saving, the family bought Mr. Egg Roll, which had a lot of work cut out for them. They had plenty of cooking and cleaning to do all day. All the kids had to pitch in after school and after they did their homework.

Once they were settled into their new home, Bà Ngoại was able to write letters to Ma back in Vietnam. She wrote about their journey to Singapore and their experience in America so far. Back in Vietnam, Ma was beyond grateful that her family made it safely to America. There was always a risk in sending the letters. But both were able to write vaguely so that Ma and Ba's family wouldn't get in trouble. Ma and Bà Ngoại were able to keep in touch, and Ma eventually told her mom about their escape plan.

After Bà Ngoại got to America, she had trouble sleeping, so she took sleeping pills. If she didn't take the pills, she would toss and turn all night worrying about her daughter back in Vietnam.

Di Minh, one of her daughters, came home from school one day and found her mom in the dining room, sitting on a chair crying. Di Minh dropped her backpack and put her arm around her mother. "What is it, Ma?" she asked.

Bà Ngoại put her hand over her heart. "I worry about Nga and her children. I miss them so much and I worry about them escaping."

Di Minh hugged her mother and tried to soothe her. "You mustn't give up hope. We'll hear from her soon. I know it."

"Nga?"

Ma shook her head and looked at the cameraman. "Sorry."

The cameraman smiled. "It's all right. I just said that I'll help you."

The man took Ma to a different tent filled with phones and typewriters. Women were behind the typewriters, their fingers flying across the keys. The room smelled of coffee and ink.

The cameraman stopped next to a woman. "Telegram," he said.

Ma frowned, and the man chuckled. "A telegram will reach your parents faster than a phone call."

"Ah," said Ma, bowing her head. "Thank you."

"Where to? Your parents, in America?" asked the man.

Ma took out a worn, folded envelope. Inside was one of the letters her mom had sent to her.

"Springfield, Missouri," Ma said, then she gave him the rest of the address, which she read from the envelope.

The woman sent the telegram, and Ma bowed and offered her thanks. The cameraman showed Ma the way back to her family and went back to the rest of his crew.

Without the help of the news crew, it would have taken months for Ma to get word out to her parents.

Bà Ngoại heard a bike bell as she sipped her tea. Then she heard footsteps and two knocks on the front door. She set down her tea, headed to the door, and opened it. A young boy with a brown cap smiled and held out an envelope.

"A telegram, ma'am."

Bà Ngoại took the envelope, bowed her head, and thanked the boy. She closed the door and sat down on the couch. Ông Ngoại came from the bathroom, rubbing his hands on his pants. He chuckled. "I'll never get used to running water." He saw the letter in Bà Ngoại's hands. "What is it?"

Bà Ngoại looked up with tears in her eyes. "It's from Nga."

Ông Ngoại sat next to his wife. "Open it."

Her hands shook and a tear fell down her cheek. "I can't."

Ông Ngoại gently took the letter from her and opened it. Bà Ngoại closed her eyes and began to pray.

"'Mr. and Mrs. Nguyen, We made it to Hong Kong. Speak soon,'" read Ông Ngoại. His voice caught, and Bà Ngoại hugged him, crying into his shirt.

"Nga made it, they finally made it," sobbed Bà Ngoại.

Ông Ngoại kissed her on the head and sighed deeply. "They really did. Soon, soon they'll be home with us."

While at Black Camp, workers came and handed food to each group. The meals, provided three times a day, were always fresh. Trucks came, and workers passed out pork, fish, rice, beef, and bread.

For Du, being at this camp was like living in jail. He had half of his freedom: everyone was allowed a certain ration of food, had a curfew, and wasn't able to do much.

The warehouse got sweltering because there were no fans and no air conditioning. The only thing that kept its occupants cool was the ocean breeze that would sneak in through the open doors and windows.

During the day, everyone was allowed to explore the camp, but when night descended, all had to return to the warehouse.

Police officers did random checks for weapons and drugs. They went through people's personal belongings and their beds to make sure nothing illegal was there. Whenever they found someone breaking the rules, they took them to a jail and sent them back to Vietnam, or they punished them by taking their valuables.

The United Nations sent money to support all the refugee camps in Hong Kong. But this wasn't the only country to receive money from the

U.N. Other countries that took in refugees from Vietnam also received funds to help keep them running.

After a couple of months at this camp, Son and his family were processed, interviewed, and approved to move to Canada.

Ba and his family still had to wait for their approval. To pass the days at camp, Ma and Tam took the children to a sand area where other kids were. They all had balls and one another to play with. The area, which was next to the beach, went up to the ocean, where the barbed-wire fence ended.

Some people had towed unwanted boats to the area so that their children could play with them.

One day, Quynh and Nhu followed older kids onto the unwanted boats.

"Be careful," called Ma.

Children laughed and chased one another around the boats. Some boys were trying to do martial arts in the corner of the play area.

Looking out at the ocean, Ma saw it was covered with boats. Boats filled with families packed on top of one another like crayons in a box. She remembered what it was like on the boat and didn't miss it. She'd hated how tight and close everyone was. No one could tell if the sweat on their body was even theirs. The sun was unbearable, turning skin red. When the wind wasn't present, Ma had tried to cool off below, but it was more humid down there. Her clothes stuck to her like glue. She got to the point where she wished she could take off her own skin to cool off.

Ma turned away from the ocean and focused on her children playing on the boats.

And there was always the BBC News crew tailing them, checking on updates and progress on their lives and getting their story.

One day when Ma was watching Quynh and Nhu playing with other kids while she rocked Dai Duong, the interviewer who helped send the telegram sat next to her.

"Hello, Mrs. Nguyen," he said. "I was wondering if I could do an interview with you?"

"Yes," said Ma, smiling.

The man returned the smile and flipped to a blank page in his journal. He took the pen from behind his ear and looked at Ma. "Thank you again for doing this."

Ma just nodded.

"Can we start from the beginning?"

Ma took a deep breath and looked off into the ocean. "We had to leave our country, our home, because of the communists. We didn't want our daughters to grow up in a place like that. We had to leave before daybreak and make our way into the darkness."

She continued telling her story—about how they made it past the shore patrol and how all seemed good until their engine broke down. With her faith in God, she didn't worry. She knew they would be saved. In the middle of the night, she gave birth to a beautiful, healthy girl. After several days stranded at sea, they came across an oil rig with wonderful men who gave them food and called for a naval ship to rescue them. The ship took them to Hainan Island, where they stayed thirteen days. Those on the island looked after them and gave them food and things to cook with, including supplies and spices. They were able to leave the island and got to Hong Kong at night. Not wanting to risk having rocks damage the boat, they waited until the sun came up.

"And that's how the police boat found us," Ma said, wrapping up the story.

The man was furiously writing, his pen flying across the page. He smiled at Ma. "And that's when we heard about your boat. When we were on the helicopter, we couldn't believe a boat like yours made it across the ocean. We were in for another surprise when we then saw the two young girls and a newborn baby."

He tentatively leaned forward. "May I ask about your experience giving birth on the boat?"

"Well, we weren't planning on having a baby on a boat," Ma said, chuckling lightly. "I had hoped we'd make it here first, but Dai Duong was ready to come into the world. Thankfully, in the end, I was fine, she was fine."

"You must have been terrified when you went to labor at sea," he said.

Ma thought back to that moment. She remembered the stiff wooden planks beneath her, darkness on either side of the boat seeming to suffocate her. There were no doctors, no nurses, looking at her with confidence and reassurance. Surrounding her was family, uncertainty deep in their eyes. For the first time giving birth, she was afraid.

Ma's hands began to shake. She folded them in front of her to keep them steady. She looked at the man and politely smiled. "I was scared, yes. But I had my family and was in God's hands."

"Wow," he said. "What an incredible ordeal."

The interviewer put his pen back behind his ear and closed his journal. "Thank you so much, Mrs. Nguyen, for your time."

Ma nodded, and he left to go back to his crew.

The next day after the interview, Ma wiped the sweat from her forehead while Ba helped the girls stand. "Let's go outside," Ba said. "Get some fresh air."

All seven went outside and squinted their eyes under the harsh sun.

"Let's go play at the park for a bit," said Ba.

They entered the sand area and were the only ones there.

"I'll race you to the boat," Quynh said to Nhu.

The girls took off and hid under a boat. Ma and Tam got closer to Ba and Du.

Ba, Ma, Tam, and Du watched the children crawl out from under the boat and tried to build sandcastles. Ba was holding Dai Duong, swaying her gently as she slept.

"What happens if they don't approve of us for resettlement? Will they send us back?" asked Du.

"They could," said Ba, wrapping an arm around Ma. "But whatever they decide, we will go through it as a family."

Du shook his head and backed away. "I can't go back. Not after all we went through."

He left the playground, and Tam went after him. Ma put an arm around Ba and moved her other toward Dai Duong. The baby opened her eyes and grasped Ma's finger.

"They'd put you back in the reeducation camps," said Ma.

Ba nodded. "They would."

If their family was rejected, Ba knew what was waiting for him back in Vietnam. Starvation, humiliation, and possibly death.

The darkest parts of his memories, which he had kept buried, were resurfacing.

Reeducation Camps

April 1975

B linded with a hood thrown over his head and his wrists handcuffed, Ba didn't know where he was being taken.

When the communists had won the war, Ba and those who had fought for the South were immediately rounded up, handcuffed, blinded, and thrown into vehicles.

Now, sitting in the back of a military van with others he had fought alongside, he clasped his hands together and thought of his family. He would do whatever it took to get back to them.

The van bumped along a road then reached its destination. The rear doors were yanked open, and Ba felt someone grab him. He was thrown out of the van and tossed like trash on the dirt road. He saw nothing but darkness. But he could still feel and hear—feel the handcuffs digging into his wrists and the scratchy hood rubbing against his skin, and hear other people being thrown from the van and the guards shouting profanities left and right just because they could.

Ba tilted his head when he heard a familiar sound. Monkeys. He realized he must be in the jungle.

Suddenly, he felt the barrel of a gun pushed up against his back. He was shoved forward. "Move," snapped a rough voice.

Ba walked forward, hearing the shuffling feet of the other men with him. He heard one of them begin to cry.

Is this it? he wondered. Had he been lied to about being reeducated on the new government? Was he being led to his death? Would darkness be the last thing he saw? Would the sobs of the man ahead of him and the curses of the guards be the last things he heard? Would the cold metal wrapped tightly around his wrists and the prickly hood over his head be the last things he felt? Or would it be a bullet?

"Halt!" shouted a voice.

Ba froze. His hands and legs began to shake. He fisted his hands to make them stop moving.

A guard ripped the hood off his head, and Ba was blinded by light. Sunlight. He blinked, adjusting his eyes, and looked around him. Other men were getting their hoods taken off as well.

In the middle of a jungle was a single reeducation camp. It was humid, and the air stuck to Ba's skin. Monkeys were above them, jumping from vine to vine and pointing down at them. They hollered as if they were laughing at the men.

Around them were small, hastily constructed cabins, with bamboo walls and thatched roofs. If no one had been around, Ba would have thought that the place was abandoned.

Men were out and about, carrying baskets of vegetables. They were wearing thin clothes, their faces smeared with sweat and dirt, hair tousled and filled with leaves. Some had chains wrapped around their ankles, which were crusted with dried blood. The guards nearby held guns or kept their hands on them in their holsters. They wore army-green clothes, hats with a red star, and shiny belt buckles.

Ba was in a long line of others who were handcuffed. At the beginning of the line was a guard who was sitting at a desk and writing down names. Each man stepped forward, provided his name, and received a set of thin, white clothes. All the men were then escorted into different buildings throughout the camp.

When it was Ba's turn, he heard a whip and someone scream. He turned and saw a guard lashing a man with bamboo. Ba forced himself to look away, but the noise continued. Other guards and prisoners who had been there longer didn't flinch; they were used to that noise by now, but those in line either looked at the man with horror or looked down at their own feet.

"Name," snapped the guard.

"Phu Nguyen," said Ba.

"Were you in the army?"

"Yes," said Ba.

The guard scribbled furiously. "Rank."

"Lieutenant," said Ba.

The whipping stopped and the screams faded.

The guard writing down the information scowled at him the whole time as if he were looking at a cockroach.

Once Ba gave all his information, he was given a brown jumpsuit and sent to a small building nearby. Inside, he was stripped of all his old clothes and possessions.

A guard with a bamboo stick swatted at Ba and the six other men in the room. "Follow me," he said.

He led them to another building. There were no windows—just a door with a lock on the outside. The guard opened the door, and Ba tried his best not to gag at the smell. It was a mixture of body odor, feces, and urine.

He and the other men were shoved inside, and the door was shut behind them. Once again, Ba was in darkness, with a little light coming from holes in the roof and slits where the standing bamboo sticks were held together. There wasn't much room in the building; it was already cramped with twenty-four other men. There were wooden beds for each person. In one corner sat a bucket for everyone to relieve themselves, and in another corner was a place where they could make a fire on cold nights.

This was now Ba's living quarters.

He wasn't sure how much time had passed since he'd arrived, but he felt himself getting weaker. Guards came only once a day to feed them scraps of food. Everyone relieved themselves in a corner, and hardly anyone spoke, afraid of what was to come.

Ba shook his head. He had never imagined his life would end up like this. He had graduated from an officer school wanting to fight for his country—and look where it got him.

How long would he have to be there? What would happen to his family? Would he ever see them again?

Eventually, the door opened and a guard entered. All the men blinked and cowered away from the sun, its bright gaze burning their eyes and bringing tears.

The guard randomly pointed at a few men and picked Ba last. "Outside," he growled.

Ba and four others stepped outside. Ba's legs trembled and ached after not being used in days. He had been doing his best in the small bamboo cabin by stretching his legs or trying to jog in place, but he was constantly bumping into people and was weakened from the lack of food.

The sun greeted him harshly. He squinted against the strong rays of light and was led to the corner of the camp where two men were tied with their hands behind them on wooden poles. Their skin was red and starting to peel. Ba swallowed hard and looked away. He and the other men were pushed down to their knees.

A guard stepped in front of them, gripping a bamboo stick. "Confess to your crimes," he said.

When Ba and the other men beside him said nothing, the guard whipped the bamboo stick right in front of their faces, almost hitting them. Ba felt a flash of cold wind in his face, but then the heat of the sun snatched it away.

"I said, confess to your crimes!" shouted the guard.

The man next to Ba opened his mouth. "I used to work for the South government."

The guard struck the man's back with the bamboo stick. The man cried out.

"Former," said the guard. "Continue."

The man panted and looked back up at the guard. "I used to work for the former South government."

The guard shook his head down at him. "You went against your own country."

The man looked down, his chin trembling. The guard took a step toward the next man, whose forehead was glistening with sweat.

"And you?" hissed the guard.

The man swallowed. "My brothers and I used to believe in and support the views of the South government. We tried to escape this country and were caught."

The guard shook his head and looked to the third man.

The third man bowed his head and said, "I used to be a Catholic. I'm here because of my past beliefs."

The fourth man looked up and stared into the guard's black eyes.

The guard frowned. "You better lower your eyes and show some respect."

The fourth man didn't falter in his gaze.

The guard whipped the bamboo stick on the man's back. "Lower those traitorous eyes and tell me why you were sent here."

"I was sent here against my will," said the man. He spat at the guard and laughed.

The guard wiped at his face, dropped the bamboo stick, and hauled the man to his feet. He ordered a nearby guard to tie the man with the men who were already tied up against wooden poles.

The guard took out a handkerchief and wiped his face. He put it back in his front pocket and picked up his bamboo stick. He used it to lift Ba's chin. "And you?"

Ba closed his eyes. "I was an officer in the former South army. I fought with the Americans."

The guard jerked the bamboo stick from under Ba's jaw and gripped the stick hard. It began to crack.

"The Americans aren't your friends. They invaded this country, and you all went against your own country. All of you, along with everyone else in this camp, will be punished and set right for your country."

Another guard came by and dropped tools in front of the men. There were two digging forks, a grubbing axe, a drag, and a draw hoe.

"Time for all of you to work for your true country," sneered the guard.

After putting his grubbing axe away, Ba tried to shrink himself against the wall as a guard walked past him clutching a letter. Ba was inside a small shed, where tools for farming and gardening were hanging on or leaning against a wall.

He took a step to follow the guard outside but noticed a small desk that had blank papers and a wooden pencil. Ba peeked out the window. Seeing no guards, just fellow prisoners, he quickly went to the desk, grabbed the pencil, and started writing. He wrote as quickly and legibly as he could.

He heard a scream and shouting outside. Ba made a mark on the page as he jumped. He looked around and back out the window. Three guards were kicking a man on the ground. The man on the ground tried to cover his head with his hands. Ba looked away from the window and finished his writing. Sweat built on his forehead as he heard the scuffling outside. He could picture himself on the ground, the guards laughing at him as they kicked his stomach, arms, and legs. He couldn't get caught; he had to do this quickly.

Ba set the pencil where he found it and folded the paper, hiding it under his armpit in his thin, brown pajama clothes. He quickly made his way to leave and found a guard standing there, his hands on his hips.

"What are you still doing here?" the guard asked, grabbing a nearby shovel and holding it above his head. "Get going!"

Ba put his hands over his head, careful with his arms so that he wouldn't drop the letter. Once Ba left the building, the guard put the shovel away and Ba went back to his sleeping quarters.

Ba—back aching, skin burning, forehead covered in sweat, clothes sticking to his skin like gum—paused in his work for a second to wipe his forehead. He was working in the cornfields. He put a hand on his shrunken stomach. Due to his lack of food, each of Ba's ribs was visible.

Ba continued with his work in the field, checking the progress of the corn plants. They were small sprouts with summer-green leaves that came up to his shin. His stomach ached as he pictured the sight of the golden-yellow kernels these plants would grow to be. His mouth watered as he imagined what they tasted like: the liquid running down his chin when he took a bite, the sweetness coating his tongue, and the emptiness he always felt in his stomach slowly being erased.

Ba shook his head, took too big of a step, and almost fell to the dirt. Around his ankles were chains. He stared at them, remembering how he had got them.

About a week earlier, with shaking arms and hands as he was completing his work for the day, Ba put away his tools and headed to his small living quarters. As he walked toward them, he sniffed the air and smelled something delicious. His stomach growled, and he followed the smell like a stray dog out in the streets. The scent was coming from the guards' quarters. A prisoner stopped in front of the door and left a basket full of potatoes.

As Ba smelled the broth in the air, his stomach twisted and turned in protest. It was acting up and needed something to soothe it. Ba stared at the potatoes, and before he knew it, his feet were walking, then he was at the basket, picking up a potato. He looked in the window. He saw three guards gathered around a table opening boxes that contained letters and packages of food. The guards sneered, kept the food in each box for themselves, and tossed the boxes and letters aside. The boxes were from captives' families. The guards were going through them, reading the letters to make sure they didn't contain anything illegal, then passing the letters out to the captives. But no one got the food from their families.

Ba stroked the potato, his fingers picking up dirt. He dusted the potato off, licked his lips, and raised it to his lips.

"How dare you," hissed a voice.

There was a snap in the air, and Ba's fingers stung. He dropped the potato and watched it roll on the ground.

A guard had come out of the building and was holding his deadly bamboo stick. He held the stick out toward Ba, pointing at him.

"It's chains for you, vermin," he growled, spit flying out of his mouth. He raised his bamboo stick and aimed for Ba's back.

Standing in the cornfield, Ba tried to clear his head of the memory of that day. Then he tried to scratch his ankles surrounded in metal. They had itched ever since he got the chains wrapped around them. All this over a potato. Ba shook his head and continued his work.

When he reached the end of a corn row, a young man walked by wearing a *nón lá*, a circular rice hat. The back of his neck and shoulders supported a long bamboo stick with rice crop hanging from both sides of the stick. He was walking without shoes on a dirt road.

Ba stepped out of the field and blocked the young man's path.

"*Chào*," greeted Ba.

The young man looked up from his walk and saw Ba.

Ba reached into his shirt and pulled out the letter he kept under his armpit. He held it out to the young man. "My name is Phu Nguyen. This is a letter for my family in Da Nang."

The young man looked Ba up and down, and when he noticed the chains around his ankles, he took a step back.

Ba went down to his knees. "No, please. I mean you no harm. I need this letter to go to my family. They don't know what happened to me. They need to know I'm alive."

The young man studied Ba, seeing every bone in his body. Ba smelled like he hadn't washed in days. His clothes had holes in them and were stained with dirt. This poor human looked like a beaten animal.

"Please," Ba begged. "Please, for my wife and two daughters."

The young man took a step forward and took the letter. "All right, Mr. Nguyen. I'll send this to your family."

"Thank you," said Ba. He got up awkwardly and bowed deeply to the young man, who could see the tears welling in Ba's eyes.

"I'm so sorry," whispered the young man. He nodded to Ba, who got out of the way so that the young man could continue walking.

Ba watched him until he was a small speck in the distance. He looked up into the clouds and as far as he could in the distance. "Please, get to my wife and children," he whispered into the wind.

The wind gently stroked his hair in response and carried leaves into the air. Ba walked back to the field and continued his work with a lighter heart. He smiled. It was going to be OK now. His family would soon know where he was.

Ba and the other captives were kept busy—getting up before the sun to work the fields and finally being able to stop once the sun set.

After months passed, the guards were more relaxed and allowed visitors into the camp. Once she learned this, Ma was determined to go visit Ba.

Getting to Ba's reeducation camp would take two bus rides—or about three to four hours—and, right after that, a motorcycle that carried passengers.

Bà Nội wanted to accompany Ma so that she could see her son. Packing light, they left when they could the afternoon after they learned they could visit. Both wanted to leave as soon as possible.

The first bus ride was stuffy and humid. People were crammed together on their way to work. Bà Nội busied herself by staring out the window. Meanwhile Ma read a book, but it was too hard for her to focus. Her thoughts kept buzzing in her head, distracting her. After the first hour, she gave up on reading and studied the people or looked out the window.

Bà Nội put her hand on top of Ma's and gave it a squeeze. "It will all be OK, Nga."

Ma smiled and looked again outside the window with Bà Nội. Ever since she had received that letter, Ma had been wondering how she would be able to see her husband again. Now there she was, on a bus after months of not seeing, hearing, or touching Ba. All that waiting and worrying—and there she was. Finally, she would see her husband at last. Finally, she would embrace him, tell him she loved him, and talk about their two daughters.

Bà Nội pointed to some people she saw in the street. "So many women alone with their children. It makes you wonder how many alongside Phu are in these camps."

The bus stopped at Hue, where they stayed the night with Bà Nội's brother.

Both women woke up early the next morning to continue on their way to see Ba. They wanted to get a good head start.

They boarded another bus and, at their destination, got off and waited for a motorcycle. They waited for only a few minutes before a motorcycle stopped in front of them.

"Where to?" asked the driver.

Bà Nội took a step closer to him and told him the location. The man nodded and gestured with his head for both to hop on. Bà Nội got on first, and Ma climbed behind her.

"Ready?" the man asked.

Bà Nội and Ma nodded. The man revved the engine and took off. The wind brought tears to their eyes and made their hair wave in the air.

The motorcycle dropped them off on a dirt road, and the rest of the journey was up to them. They had to get through a swamp, half the time walking through warm, muddy water and the other half climbing up hills, swatting at any bugs that came near. The monkeys howled above and swung from the vines. Echoing in the jungle were the sounds of elephants trumpeting.

After they made it through the swamp, ahead in the distance was the camp. Bà Nội and Ma shared a smile and continued on, getting closer and closer.

As they neared the gates, two guards straightened their pose and held out their guns to make them obvious. Ma swallowed nervously while Bà Nội patted her hand and walked up to one of the guards.

"Excuse me," said Bà Nội. "I'm here to see my son."

Ma eyed the ten-foot bamboo fence that surrounded the camp, as well as the barbed wire at the top to stop people from escaping.

The guard opened the door and let Ma and Bà Nội in. The guard pointed to a nearby office. "In there."

Bà Nội walked as fast as she could, her eyes locked on the office. Ma staggered behind, the smell of bodily fluids making her bring a hand over her nose. She looked around, trying to see if she could see Ba. Those she glanced at looked like they hadn't showered in years. Their faces were covered in sweat and dirt, flies buzzing above them, and their pajama-like clothes were black and full of holes. Some men were on the ground, lying so still that had their chests not been moving up and down, Ma would have thought they were dead.

"Nga," called Bà Nội.

Ma went inside the office with Bà Nội. It was small and formal. There was a desk, behind which was a window left open to let some wind in. The desk was carefully looked after. There were papers and journals stacked on top of each other in neat rows, three pens laid next to each other, and a framed picture of Ho Chi Minh.

Ba's close friend from high school limped past the office and glanced inside. He paused in his walk, seeing two familiar faces. He turned the opposite direction and ran for the fields, running as fast and as best as he could with a hurt foot.

Back in the office, a man was standing behind a desk.

"Hello. How may I help you?" he asked. "Please, sit down."

Ma and Bà Nội sat on chairs opposite the man. He, too, sat down, then flipped over some papers to hide what he had been writing.

"We came to see Phu Nguyen," said Bà Nội.

"Of course. One moment," said the guard. He wrote the name down and stood. "Someone will come and escort you to the visiting cabin."

He left, and a guard came five minutes later. He bowed in greeting. "I'm here to take you both to the visiting cabin. Please, follow me."

Bà Nội and Ma followed him outside. Bà Nội squinted her eyes against the sun while Ma lifted her hand to shade her eyes.

They followed the guard to the cabin. Looking around, they saw that the men they. had seen earlier were all gone.

When visitors came, the guards would tell half the men to go to their living quarters while the other half were forced to wait in the jungle.

Ma and Bà Nội entered the cabin. A man inside was hastily dusting. When he saw the guard and the two women, he gasped and quickly left.

Inside the room was a couch facing two armchairs. In the middle was a coffee table made of wood. On top of that was a tray that had a pitcher of water and mismatched cups. On one wall hung a huge oil painting of a rice field, and on the other wall was a big window with a view of the jungle.

"Please, wait here," said the guard. He closed the door behind him while Ma and Bà Nội went to the couch and waited.

Out in the field, Ba's friend stopped in front of Ba, who was working. Ba's friend bent over and started panting. "Family. Yours. Here."

Ba dropped a piece of corn and started running toward the camp. He stopped and turned around to his friend. "Where?"

"Cabin," his friend panted. "Visiting cabin."

Ba ran as fast as he could, the thought of his family there giving him a new sense of urgency. He ran to the visiting cabin and threw the doors open. Ma and Bà Nội stood and faced the door.

Ba's throat tightened and tears came to his eyes. "Nga! Mother!"

He ran to them, and Bà Nội and Ma ran to him. The three met halfway.

Ba forgot about the hunger and the pain from his fresh wounds. All he could see was his family, and he felt whole again.

He gathered both of them in a hug. Bà Nội and Ma hugged back, and the three of them stood there putting all their love into their arms, hoping one another could feel it.

Ba pulled back and looked at his wife. "You're still here? I thought you would have tried to escape with your family once the war was lost. I thought you'd be far away from here."

Tears came to Ma's eyes. She put a hand to his cheek and shook her head. "I tried, but I couldn't leave you behind. I couldn't. You're my family, too."

Ba rested his forehead against hers.

Bà Nội was alarmed by Ba's appearance. Her son looked malnourished, weak, and exhausted. But she was grateful to see him alive.

Ma and Bà Nội were allowed to stay there for the night. They were shown to a room filled with single beds for visitors. The mattresses were cheap, and there were no pillows to rest one's head.

After their first visit, Ma and Bà Nội were allowed to come back every three months to visit Ba. Sometimes they would bring Nhu and Quynh, still too young to understand why their father couldn't come home and where he truly was.

For three years, Ba lived at this reeducation camp. For three years, he went out to the fields to grow and collect corn. For three years, he was starved and felt trapped. The guards rarely hit—neither with their sticks nor with their fists. They used hunger against the prisoners at camp. If the captives did what they were told, they were fed—but never fed enough. They were mostly fed scraps, a hundred grams of meat, a hundred grams of sugar, and sometimes even two slices of sweet potato once a day. Just enough food to give them energy to work ten-hour shifts daily. Only on holidays did the guards give more food than usual, and they were nice enough to hand people packages filled with food that their families had sent them on holidays only.

Ba witnessed fellow prisoners get so hungry that they ate bugs, such as cockroaches and ants. He even saw people get desperate enough to eat mushrooms and rats. Those who ate the mushrooms and the rats got sick. Some even died.

Those who couldn't take it anymore made a run for the jungle, taking with them the clothes on their back and a weapon—the shovel or pickax they had in their hands—or no tool at all. Others would watch and never see those men again. No one knew if they met their demise in the jungle or if they were able to escape its depths.

Living in these camps, Ba and his fellow captives felt like animals. They were hungry all the time and numb. Around the clock, all they thought about was food. The guards used that to their advantage: when the captives worked, they received food. It wasn't the guards' intention for any of the men at camp to die. They wanted all the men to be alive, just enough to be able to keep working.

If Ba wasn't out working in the fields, he helped cut down trees. Guards sold the wood. Or he broke apart rocks with tools to create more land to plant vegetables. Not once were those imprisoned in the camp paid for their hard work.

Sometimes men at camp had their own firewood. During the cold nights, in a corner of Ba's cabin, they used the firewood they were allowed to keep. They'd start fires to beat back the cold.

The only cemetery in the camp grew bigger and bigger every day. Bodies that were to be buried piled up near the entrance. Those in the body pile had died from starvation, the cold, or disease.

Every day, Ba had to pass the cemetery, watching his fellow captives digging holes for the dead. He did his best to not look at the faces of the dead, but the longer he stayed, the more he would peek and stare. He'd look at the faces, seeing if one was familiar. He'd stare long enough until he saw his own face.

He began to wonder what it would be like to go to sleep and never wake up in this life, in this body. *Would I wake up and be reborn*, he wondered. *This past life just a memory? Or would I escape the cycle of samsara, the cycle of repetitive birth, death and rebirth caused by karma, and finally reach nirvana, a state of enlightenment?*

When Ba's family visited him, the darkness that had been hanging over his head vanished and was replaced with light. His thoughts of rebirth or eternal peace disappeared. He realized he couldn't die. Not like this in this life. His life was only beginning. Looking at his daughters' smiles and his wife's eyes, he couldn't have it end like this. He had to keep going. But every time his family left, they took the light with them. And it was getting harder and harder to envision a better end.

Every New Year's Eve, Ba and the other prisoners would stare upward and watch the fireworks. They were always a great distraction and yet, as he looked up at their bright colors, Ba's heart ached. He wished he could experience this moment with his family. Wished he could take them to the dragon dances, eat as much as his stomach could take, and prepare the red envelopes, stuffing them with lucky money and giving them to his girls.

When the fireworks ended, Ba and the others were once again in darkness.

While Ba was at camp, his family had to live with the start of communism.

Each family was given a ticket that allowed them to enter a warehouse daily. Once there, every family could get only a certain ration of rice and other foods. But that wasn't enough for some families.

Famine began to spread through the land, and Ma and Bà Nội's family didn't receive enough food to feed them all. The only food they got was bad-quality stuff. Their family got as skinny as Ba while he was at camp.

Quynh and her cousin Thuy started kindergarten. They'd wake up at six in the morning and be on their way to school, which started at eight and ended at four in the afternoon. Lunch ran for two hours, starting at noon. School was very strict. Teachers wanted their students to recite their lessons, write everything down, and memorize all of it. If a student forgot or stumbled when reciting what they learned, they were punished with a spanking.

When communism took over, boys who were at least eighteen could be drafted if they failed in school, or if they had a family member who tried to escape or was—or had been—in the reeducation camps.

Ba would have probably stayed at the camp longer than three years, but he had an uncle who was connected with the communist government and was able to get Ba released early.

The day Ba was released from the reeducation camp, his family was there waiting for him at the front gates. He kissed his mom on the forehead and his wife on the cheek. He went down on his knees to hug his children. Both embraced him with their small arms.

Ba had tears come to his eyes. He blinked them away and stood.

"Let's get you home," said Bà Nội.

Home, thought Ba.

It had been so long since he had walked through his own home, slept in a comfortable bed, and heard in the background the sound of his children instead of the screams and cries of the men around him in camp.

When they all arrived at home, he looked at the house, seeing the familiar tailor shop below. He smiled at the banana and papaya trees. Ma pulled on his hand, and he entered his house for the first time in three years. Tears came to his eyes, and he quickly blinked them away— he didn't want his family to see him cry. The girls skipped into the house and headed to their room.

Ma hugged Ba's arm and kissed his shoulder. "Welcome home."

It felt like home for the first couple of days. But it slowly began to feel like a prison. Ba was required every week to report to the new government; in his report was a log of his daily activities.

Even though he was with his family, Ba felt trapped, felt like he was in that camp with all those other men, because his actions were still being closely monitored. His family, too, was starving.

When he was in that camp, Ba feared communism, and a hatred grew deep in his belly every time a guard gave him little food. His heart shattered into a million pieces once communist leaders began imposing their ideology and social structure on his family and friends.

Holding a cigarette in one hand and a glass of rice wine in the other, Ba sat on a bench on the front porch when Ma came outside and sat next to him after she tucked in the kids. Hanging from the porch ceiling was a bamboo chime that was still. There was no wind that night to play music. Birds sang their final goodnight songs and were black shadows flying in the night. It had been about a month since Ba's release from the reeducation camps.

"What's wrong?" asked Ma.

Ba took a sip of the rice wine. "I fear for our future and, most importantly, our children. They can't have a future here."

"What are you saying?" whispered Ma.

Ba put the cigarette in his mouth and inhaled, the embers flickering at the end. "I mean," he said, blowing smoke into the air, "I don't want to raise our children here. We can't live like this anymore."

"Even if we could leave," Ma said, "where would we go? They'll catch you if you try to escape."

"We'll follow in your parents' footsteps. Go to America."

Ma thought of her parents and siblings. It would be nice to see them again, give them a chance to see their grandkids, and have her children grow up in a country that could provide them a better life than Vietnam could. "But ... How?" whispered Ma. She leaned on his chest, and Ba set his glass down to wrap his arm around her.

"Don't you worry about it. I'll think of something," Ba said. "But I promise you, we will find a way to escape and give our kids the life they deserve."

Chi Ma Wan Camp

July 30, 1979

On the last day at Black Camp for Ba and the others, they were ushered to a van that would take them to a different camp, Chi Ma Wan. Since Ba and his family were having their paperwork processed, it was best to move them to a different camp. Dozens of new refugees came every day to Black Camp, so space was needed.

Residing at Chi Ma Wan Camp were five thousand refugees, all waiting to be approved to begin a new life in a sponsoring country.

Their new living quarters were in another warehouse with two hundred rows of metal bunk beds. In each building, four hundred refugees slept. Families were spread out, some hanging wet laundry on the bunk beds, others putting up flower-printed sheets to give themselves as much privacy as possible.

An officer escorted Ba and his family toward the back of the warehouse to their designated area.

Quynh and Nhu went to their shared bunk bed and climbed the ladder excitedly.

Ba laughed. "You two can sleep on the top bunk."

"Yippy!" cried Quynh.

Ba helped Nhu and both girls lie down on their new bed.

They stayed at Chi Ma Wan Camp for four months.

Refugees could leave the camp, but they needed permission. Even so, not a lot of people were permitted to leave even when asking for permission. Ba, Du, and Tam got permission to leave camp to find jobs and earn money. There were a lot of manufacturing companies nearby. Ba and Du were lucky enough to find work at a company that made toys. Tam found a job sewing clothes. The only person who didn't work was Ma, who stayed with the girls. She watched over her newborn and took the girls to a nearby playground. Ma and Tam cooked breakfast, and afterward, Ba, Du, and Tam took the bus to work. After playing all morning each day, Ma made the girls lunch, and they'd wait in the warehouse until Tam got back from work. They'd cook dinner for the men when they got back from the toy building, and all would go for a walk around camp.

At the nearby docks, food supplies arrived twice a week. People came out of the warehouse, helped unload all the food, and lined up to get their ration for the day. There was fresh fish, rice, eggs, chicken wings, oranges, vegetable oil, ground beef, ground pork, and vegetables. There were no scales to divide the food, so everyone divided the food as equally as possible for four hundred people. No one knew what the beef was, but Ba just took it. They stored food under their bunk beds, and whenever they cooked, they did so outside over a fire. Ba and Ma went to the nearby families and asked if they could borrow their pots and pans.

Just outside their building there was an area where some people who had been there for months or years grew their own fruits and vegetables. Potatoes unburied themselves from the ground, onions grew like heads poking out from deep in the ground, and ripe tomatoes blushed red, ready to be plucked. There were also trees growing mangoes, pomegranates, and dates. Those who owned their little plot of land sold their vegetables and fruits to other refugees or ate the produce themselves.

After working enough, Ba was able to buy a portable stove and a rice cooker.

Slowly, everyone gained their weight back and became less hungry. They forgot what it was like to starve, with their stomachs growling and shrinking in size. Now their stomachs grew, and after every meal, all were satisfied.

One afternoon, Ba and Du went to downtown Hong Kong. They were going to track down their Uncle Bay, who had left three months before them. Uncle Bay was at Jubilee, another refugee camp.

Ba and Du pointed at the cars, never seeing such fast machines go by in streams of red, yellow, and black. They roared, sounding as territorial as lions and tigers. Other cars slowed down or got out of the way to let these monster machines pass. The buildings towered above like giants. Ba had never felt so small in his life.

Once they reached Jubilee, Du and Ba split up and promised to meet back at the entrance in an hour. The refugees at this camp were out and about. Children were laughing and playing Wing Chun, a form of kung fu, together out in a field—or, at least, they were trying to play it. At that age, a lot of them had not mastered it and couldn't hold their balance when playing. People were gathered around together talking or seeking shade under the trees.

Ba and Du went into a building and split up the floor levels between them. They knocked on every door and asked for their uncle.

As Ba walked through the halls, a boy about ten years old was stumbling down the hallway and ran into Ba.

"S- Sorry," the young boy stuttered.

Ba helped the boy up and was hit with the smell of alcohol. "Where are your parents?" asked Ba.

The boy, who had clouded eyes, pushed him away and continued stumbling down the hall. "I'm an orphan," he called out.

Ba watched the boy, then continued to look for Uncle Bay.

When Ba was ready to leave a room after an hour into his search, his uncle came out from a bathroom, wiping his hands on his pants. Ba and Uncle Bay bowed and tightly hugged each other.

"So glad to see you made it," said Uncle Bay. "Sit down."

Both sat on a nearby bed.

"Tell me your story," said Uncle Bay.

Ba smiled and told his tale about his family and the three other families he had traveled with.

"I'm so glad you and the rest of your family made it." Uncle Bay shook his head in disbelief. "It's the Lord's work on your family getting here. Unbelievable. Your story is one of the few I've heard that ended on a happy note. Anyway, is there anything I can do for you?"

"I need to borrow some money to contact Nga's mother in America, and to buy some pots and pans and clothes for the girls."

Uncle Bay went to his bed and grabbed a bag from under it. He unzipped it. "How much?"

Ba sighed. "Three hundred."

Uncle Bay took out the money with no hesitation and put it in a sock. He handed it to Ba.

Ba bowed deeply. "I'll pay you back when I can."

Uncle Bay smiled. "No worries."

Ba bowed again and put the sock in his pocket. "Thank you, Uncle. I hope I brought joy to your day."

Uncle Bay laughed, and they both bowed. "You got me to laugh. Something I haven't done in a while."

"I'll see you around, Uncle."

"Give my blessings to the rest of the family," said Uncle Bay.

Ba went back to the entrance where Du waited, leaning against the front gate with his arms crossed.

"I found him," said Ba. "Let's go find a phone."

Du and Ba left Jubilee and walked the streets. They found a post office, which had public phones.

As Ba went to the front desk, Du browsed through the store, looking at the paper and writing utensils. Ba paid ten dollars to make a phone call. He pulled out a letter that Bà Ngoại had written to Ma and saw the telephone number circled at the bottom. Ba dialed the number, held the phone to his ear, and heard it ring. He bit his lip. It was two in the afternoon in Hong Kong and two in the morning in Missouri.

Another set of rings went by. Ba closed his eyes and held his breath. "Please answer," he whispered.

"Hello?"

Ba sighed in relief. "Hello, it's Phu."

"Phu, oh my Lord," Bà Ngoại said with excitement. "Where's Nga?"

"She's at camp. I wanted to give you our address. We're at Chi Ma Wan Camp now." He listed off the rest of the address he had gotten earlier from a police officer.

"It's so good to hear from you, Phu. Take care of my daughter and granddaughters."

"I will. We'll talk again soon."

He kept the call short because long-distance international calls cost a lot of money.

Du saw Ba hang up the phone and walked back to him. Ba patted his pocket. "Let's go shopping."

Du and Ba went to some stores. They got a suitcase, a portable stovetop, two pans, bowls, chopsticks, women's underwear, and men's shorts. For the children, Ba got candy, such as White Rabbit and ice jelly. And butter cookies and raisin oat cookies. Finally, three outfits each for Quynh and Nhu.

On the way back to camp, they passed children rummaging through trash cans and picking up empty soda cans. The children were searching in the trash for anything valuable they could sell. Du, who had gotten a soda from a shop, went up to a girl with her black hair in a braid. Her dress was tattered and her stomach was protruding. Du forced a smile and handed her his empty soda can. "Here."

The girl smiled and took the can. She bowed and put a hand on her belly.

"How old are you?" Du asked her.

"Thirteen," she said.

Ba dug into a plastic bag and took out a cookie. He held it out to her. She bowed again and took the cookie. She nearly swallowed the whole thing.

"Where are your parents?" asked Ba.

The girl's face fell. She turned and ran off, following the other children.

"Wait," called Du.

Ba and Du didn't follow her, not wanting to frighten her. Ba put a hand on Du's shoulder. "Come. There's nothing we can do."

Du stood for a few minutes waiting for the little girl to come back around the corner. But she never did.

A week later, Bà Ngoại sent out a money order for five hundred dollars. Every U.S. dollar was worth five Hong Kong dollars.

Ba and Du took a ferry and went back to downtown Hong Kong. They found an American Express bank and exchanged the U.S. dollars for Hong Kong dollars.

With that money, Ba bought a Vietnam driver's license and went back to Jubilee Camp to repay their uncle.

Du and Ba found Uncle Bay outside, smoking and sitting on a chair, watching the children feeding seeds to the birds.

Ba held out three hundred dollars in Hong Kong currency. "Here. Thank you again."

Uncle Bay gently pushed back Ba's hand. "You keep it. It was a gift. There's no need to repay me. We're family."

Ba smiled. "Thank you, Uncle. Bless you."

After visiting their uncle for a while, Ba and Du left the camp.

On their way out, they passed a building filled with orphans. Some of the teenage girls were pregnant, and the boys were getting drunk in a corner.

Ba shook his head and looked at Du. "I wish they would take care of the orphans here."

Du looked at the kids and nodded in agreement.

"Before we head back home, I need to get a Philips radio, to hear the news," said Ba.

"OK," said Du.

Hong Kong was a huge city, with tall buildings rocketing to the sky. The streets were busy, filled with people coming and going to their jobs or their homes. Ba and Du went to many electronics stores, trying to find a Philips radio. It had to be a Philips because Ba liked the name and had heard it was a reliable brand.

As the sun was starting to set, they found another store and asked if they had a Philips radio.

"We sure do," said the owner. He went to the back of his store and came back with a Philips radio. "Fifty dollars. You can plug it into an outlet or put in some batteries to make it work." The owner set the radio on the counter and took out a case. "It also comes with this nice carrying case."

Ba looked it over and nodded. "We'll take it."

Before they headed back to camp, they stopped to buy some chocolates for the girls and cigarettes for Ba.

Ba woke up in the middle of the night with sweat in the middle of his back and across his forehead. He was panting and his heart was racing. He remembered gunshots, running in the jungle, monkeys screaming above him, and a hot, searing pain coming from his leg.

He rolled up his left pant leg and ran his fingers over his bullet-wound scar.

"What happened?" whispered a sleepy voice.

Ba looked up and saw that Quynh had gotten down from the top bunk. Her head was tilted to the side, her dark-brown hair in a tangled mess. Ba opened his right arm and Quynh went into it. She pointed at his leg.

"Is it like your other scar? On your arm?"

Ba covered up his leg and helped Quynh lie beside him. "Yes."

"Does it hurt?"

Ba shook his head. "No."

"Do you have any more?"

Ba uncovered his left arm, showing two bullet scars.

"Did the same person hurt you?" whispered Quynh. She pointed at his arm. "You said someone hurt you."

"Don't worry, my daughter. They can't hurt me anymore, not from here," said Ba.

"Is that why we had to leave home?"

"Yes," said Ba. "And for other reasons I'll tell you when you're older."

Quynh buried her face in the pillow and mumbled something.

"What was that?" asked Ba. He gently rolled her on her back and saw tears in her eyes. "What's wrong?"

"I miss home. I miss Bà Nội," she said, referring to Ba's mother.

Ba held Quynh against his chest. "It's OK to miss home and your bà nội . I miss her, too."

"Will we ever get to go back?"

Ba sighed into her hair and shrugged. "I don't know. Maybe when you're older or when the country gets better. Now sleep. Try to get some sleep."

Quynh sniffled and closed her eyes. Ba also closed his eyes, and this time he dreamed of how the jungle was before the war. Before blood seeped into the earth, before the birds were cawing desperately and going as fast as their wings could carry them. Before silence knew the damage of war.

What home used to look and feel like.

Two weeks passed, and Bà Ngoại sent more money their way. A fifty-dollar check. Muh Vinh, Bà Ngoại's sister, also sent a check—another fifty dollars.

Ba went to a jewelry store and asked if they could cash it.

The man behind the counter lifted an eyebrow and looked at the letter. He saw the U.S. stamp and knew it wasn't a fake. "OK, we'll cash it."

Heading back to the warehouse, Ba passed a graveyard. Two men were digging a hole. A young couple were hugging each other and crying. Ba saw one of the men pick up a small casket and place it gently in the hole.

Ba went to the men and took one of the shovels. He helped them cover the hole. The young couple saw this and walked over when the hole was covered.

"Thank you, sir," said the young man.

The woman wiped her cheeks, and Ba smiled gently. "I'm sorry for your loss," he said. Ba left the couple to grieve and hugged his daughters tighter when he put them to bed that night.

September brought the Chongyang festival, a holiday celebrated in Hong Kong. On that day, locals ate chongyang cake, drank chrysanthemum wine, climbed mountains, and paid homage to chrysanthemums.

The staff at camp wanted the refugees to be involved with the holiday. Women passed out chrysanthemums to the children. Nhu dipped her nose in a red one, and Quynh put a yellow one behind her ear.

For dinner, staff gave each adult a glass of chrysanthemum wine, and for dessert, they gave everyone a slice of chongyang cake.

Quynh and Nhu each took a bite of the cake.

"What do you think?" asked Ba. He held his piece of cake out in front of him and made a face. "Should I eat it?"

The girls giggled and nodded.

"It's really good," said Quynh.

"Delicious," said Nhu.

Ba went to take a bite but paused. He looked back to his daughters. "Are you sure? You're not tricking me?"

The girls laughed and shook their heads. Ba took a bite and smiled. Almonds, jujube, and chestnuts coated Ba's tongue. "You're right. This tastes good." He finished before the girls and tried to sneak a piece from their plates.

Ma smiled at the scene and wanted more than anything for this moment to last forever.

In order for his family to be able to get to America, Ba had to fill out a lengthy application form. This form could also be used to live in Canada, France, Germany, Sweden, or Australia. While filling out paperwork, it took Ba a couple of hours to try to translate and understand the papers written in English. He asked Cau Hoang, one of Ma's brothers, to send them an English dictionary so he could fill out the papers faster.

On the forms, Ba wrote that Nga's mother already lived in America and that he had once been a military officer. Ma was appointed head of the household since her family was in America. After learning this, refugee-relocation officials moved their application higher on the priority list.

Ba finally handed over that paperwork, as well as personal documents, such as everyone's birth certificates and IDs. The woman who took it all copied the paperwork and handed it back to Ba. "Thank you," she said. "We'll call you in ten days."

There was nothing else Ba could do but wait for the approval on their application—an approval that would bring them a step closer to a new life.

After about three months, their application was finally approved by immigration officials, but it would take a couple months before they could actually leave. In the meantime, their health had to be checked out and more paperwork needed to be done.

Each year, only a certain number of refugees were allowed into various countries. The U.S. government sent immigration officials to refugee camps to make sure visa applications were correct and that everyone seeking to come to America was legitimate and that their paperwork didn't look suspicious.

One night, as Ba and Du headed to their warehouse, they passed a building. Ba peeked inside and saw a group of people sitting in chairs in a circle. Usually, this room was used for entertainment. They would set up a stage and have a band play, inviting people to come and dance.

Candles were lit on a back table that was filled with snacks and drinks. There were crackers, meat and cheese slices, and fruit. There was water and tea next to some clay cups.

An old woman was by the door and saw Ba peeking in. "Would you like to join us?" she asked.

"What are you guys doing?" asked Du.

"We're telling our stories of how we got here. You're more than welcome to come in." The woman pointed at a back table. "There are some snacks there, and I'll go get extra chairs."

Ba followed her to the extra chairs while Du got some snacks and tea. Ba grabbed two chairs, and the group of people made room and stopped talking.

As they joined the group, Du handed Ba some tea.

"Sorry, we didn't mean to interrupt," said Ba.

"That's all right," said a woman. She looked at a man and nodded at him. "You may continue."

The man shuffled his fingers in his lap. "So, as I was saying, I didn't want to lose my great-grandmother's ring. It was the only thing left I had of my family. As the pirates were stealing jewelry from other people, I made a quick decision. I swallowed the ring. But I swallowed it wrong. It got stuck. I tried not to panic, and then the pirate moved on to me. He opened my mouth forcefully and looked everywhere." The man pulled out a necklace from under his shirt, and hanging from the necklace was a ring "Thankfully, they didn't find it."

Everyone clapped politely.

"Thank you, Thrang. I'm so happy you were able to keep that ring. And even more happy that you're here with us," said the woman. She turned to Ba and Du, who were sipping their tea. "My name is Sophie. I'm from America and have come to volunteer. I started these meetings to help people tell their stories or listen to others' stories on how they got here."

"I'm Phu, and this is my brother Du," said Ba.

Everyone greeted and welcomed them. Then the woman looked around the circle. "Who would like to go next?" she asked.

Everyone looked around until two sisters raised their hands.

"My name is Hue," one of the two said, "and this is my sister Yen. We were the first of our family to escape."

Ba listened to their story of miraculously getting away from pirates, being shot at, and finally making it to Hong Kong.

Others told less-fortunate stories. Stories of being attacked by pirates. Pirates who stole their jewelry, wedding rings, and family heirlooms. Pirates who separated the men from the women, making everyone take off their clothes so that the pirates could search for valuables and take advantage of the women, raping them for days. Pirates who forced people's mouths open and removed their gold teeth with pliers. Others told a rare story about pirates taking all their belongings, and before leaving, tossing the boat people some leftover food they had.

Parents told stories of losing their children on the way there. Children going overboard, children dying of starvation, or catching an illness and dying at the camp. Some parents had to send their children off so they could try to have a better life than the one they had in Vietnam. Parents had only two choices: send their children off in boats to live a better life or see their children being sent off to fight a war in Cambodia at a young age. The parents either carried guilt when they never heard from their children again or felt blessed to be reunited with them. Mothers cried when they told how they had to give children their own urine to drink to be able to keep them going.

People told stories of watching people of all ages—from elders to babies—dying on the boat, getting lost at sea, catching diseases, or dying from lack of food or water. What hurt most of all was going all that way to camp only to lose someone there.

In most stories, people had been lied to and cheated. When families or individuals looked for boats to escape in, they ended up paying their life savings, only to find no boat in sight when they arrived at the ocean. That was when they realized they had been scammed.

Finally, after many stories had been shared, Sophie stood. "I want to thank you all for coming," she said. "We'll have this same meeting next week at the same time. Please, invite others to come."

Five days later, the next holiday in Hong Kong arrived. The event, called the Mid-Autumn Festival, ran for a week. The streets throughout downtown were decorated with lanterns. Children were given small ones, and they ran down the gravel roads like comets in the sky.

Ba and Du went into downtown Hong Kong. Both were mesmerized by all the lights, sounds, and colors. The crowd parted for the lion dance to take place. People were dressed in costumes of yellow, white, pink, and orange. Performers in lion costumes danced along to drums and cymbals.

A white lion stood before several poles sprouting from the ground. Its black eyes blinked under bushy eyebrows, and it opened its wide mouth as if it was going to swallow the closest person. The performers brought the lions to life. They jumped, glided, and flew above the poles as if they never touched the ground. The wind seemed to levitate them, as if gravity weren't fighting against them. People in the crowd cheered and clapped, including Ba and Du.

Ba leaned toward Du's ear. "Let's go get some treats for the family."

Du nodded and followed Ba along the streets. They passed people clothed in bright colors and passed children chasing one another like lions. The smell of crab and other seafood delicacies filled the air, making people sniff the air like dogs. The most popular treats being sold were moon cakes.

On the way back to their family, Ba and Du ate their moon cakes. Red-bean paste and lotus-seed paste filled their mouths. When Du was done, he licked his fingers and rubbed his belly.

When Ba gave the girls, Ma, and Tam the moon cakes, he was able to get some ginger tea in Hong Kong and share it with his family. While the girls ate, Ba and Du demonstrated as best they could the lion dance. The girls' eyes were wide, and they gasped.

"I wish I could have seen it," said Quynh.

"Me, too," said Nhu.

Ba sat between them. "Don't worry, my daughters. You still have plenty to see."

"Yes, we'll be going to America. A place not a lot of people from our country have been able to go to," said Ma. "We'll have a lot to see when we get there."

"Like what?" asked Quynh as she finished her moon cake.

Ba thought for a moment. "Snow."

Quynh widened her eyes. "Snow?"

"Yes. America has snow, and it gets very cold. Something we're all not used to."

"What else?" Nhu excitedly asked. She ate the last bite of her moon cake, with some lotus paste on her nose.

"They have this tall statue. It's called the Statue of Liberty. It's green and in a place called New York. Kind of like Hong Kong, with all of its tall buildings spread out for miles and miles."

"More, tell us more," said Quynh.

Ba laughed and told them about many popular monuments and places in America that his girls could see there.

Camp Jubilee

November 30, 1979

Four months later, they were moved again—this time to Camp Jubilee. It took a bus and a ferry ride to get there.

Ba and Du, who had become familiar with the camp when they saw their uncle there, knew where everything was and felt comfortable. Their uncle was no longer at the camp. He was able to get his paperwork processed and approved, and he was sent to start his life in America.

Jubilee was a former military base. Each room, with bunk beds, was assigned to two families and could fit up to twenty people. Ma and Ba's group shared a room with another family that included a man, his wife, and their three children. The room had windows that were cracked open to let in a refreshing breeze. Clothes were left hanging on the bunk beds to dry. The room was spacious, and everyone was able to have their own bed.

Ba and his family had more freedom in this camp than in the previous ones. The people seemed happier. They smiled more and the children laughed more. There were huge gardens outside with birds flying high above. The weather had cooled off; it wasn't stifling hot. The camp was loud and noisy, with people chatting above one another in good spirits.

Every night at ten, the gates closed. They reopened at five or six the next morning. Those in camp were allowed to leave and go to work. When they were able to find work, they met nice people who treated them kindly.

Two times a day, a big truck brought food—enough for all and always different, so no one ate the same thing twice. Cooking wasn't allowed, so everyone relied on the truck.

There were also churches spread throughout the camp, along with Buddhist shrines surrounded by beautifully lush gardens, a medical center, a school for children, a therapy facility, and a safe place for the children to play.

Each morning after breakfast, Ma and Tam dropped off the girls at school so they could get an education. They came back for the girls at lunch and took them to the park. Nhu and Quynh learned and sang songs, and they were able to draw with crayons and paint on canvases.

A lot of people from Hong Kong and other countries donated toys and school supplies for the kids.

Ma visited the church at least once a week to listen to sermons, pray with others, or sit in silence with her fellow Catholics.

Ba often visited the Buddhist shrine. He sat among the forget-me-nots and yellow-mustard flowers, shaded by lychee and knema trees. Birds chirped peacefully, and the wind blew soothingly.

At this new camp, Ba assisted other fellow refugees with their paperwork because many didn't know English. Thanks to some English he knew and the English dictionary, he was able to help others with their applications.

One man Ba helped held out some money for him. Ba shook his head and gently pushed the man's hand away. "No. You keep. My pleasure to help." Others, too, wanted to pay Ba money, but he always refused. So instead of money, they paid him with cigarettes, candy, cookies, oranges, and apples.

Before Christmas arrived, Ma and Ba went downtown to find gifts for the family. Ma bought Chinese tea, pinwheels, a temple charm, dim sum, and milk pudding. She went to church to celebrate the birth of Jesus. Sometimes, the girls would join her; other times, they would go to the Buddhist temple with Ba.

On Christmas Day, the girls opened their pinwheels, Ba thanked Ma for the temple charm, and Tam and Du loved the Chinese tea and dim sum. The camp served roast turkey. After a full meal, they headed back to their bunk beds and were given milk pudding.

Ma tucked the girls in. She kissed their heads and whispered into their hair how blessed she was to have them. Before she fell asleep, she thanked God for getting them where they were and asked Him to continue helping them meet up with her family in America.

The next day, after hanging outside all day and celebrating, the family was heading back to their sleeping quarters when there was a bang and colors exploded in the night sky.

The girls looked up and gasped.

Fireworks in red, white, green, blue, and purple painted the black sky.

Nhu lifted her arms in front of Ba. "Higher, Ba. I want to try to touch the fireworks."

Ba chuckled and lifted Nhu around his neck. Du did the same for Quynh. The girls clapped and shouted in glee at the fireworks. Ma and Tam headed back to their beds. Dai Duong was crying. Ma hoped that by the time they got to their beds, Dai Duong wouldn't be able to hear the fireworks and would be able to go to sleep.

After the fireworks show, the men set the girls back down on the ground.

"Let's get you to bed," said Ba.

The girls pouted. "Can't we stay up a little bit longer?"

Ba grabbed his daughters' hands and led them back to their beds. "Sorry, girls. It's time for bed."

They returned to their beds, where Dai Duong was sound asleep. Tam, too, was asleep. The only one awake was Ma. She smiled as her family walked in.

After Ba got the girls into bed, he held out his hand to Ma. "Come on."

Ma tilted her head to the side. "Where are we going?" She took his hand.

Ba tugged at her hand and led her outside. "It's a surprise."

He took Ma to a building music was coming from. Other families and friends had gathered to celebrate New Year's. Music played in the background and people danced in a circle.

Ba bowed to Ma. "Shall we dance?"

Ma pulled Ba to the dance floor and laughed. They did the cha-cha, their favorite dance.

Two months had passed since they arrived at Camp Jubilee. Everyone was adjusting to day-to-day activities while optimistically waiting to hear from immigration officials on the status of their paperwork. Ma prayed every day that they would receive their permit to settle in the United States and be reunited with her parents and siblings. If an applicant had parents, children, or a spouse already living in the United States, their chance of admission increased. Other families were also waiting for approval from a handful of other countries that accepted refugees.

Once a month, Bà Ngoại sent money. Ba used it to buy cigarettes, beer on occasion, and disposable diapers.

At their new camp, there were classes on different subjects, including life in America. These classes helped refugees prepare for settlement in a new country. There were classes on American manners, sports, movies, games, holidays, health/medical, vocations, the library, postal services, arts and crafts, typing, tailoring, and religious programs. There were classes on what it would be like to fly on a plane, as well as what electronics and machines were like in America and how to operate them. There were also English classes. Refugees could learn different musical instruments, such as guitar, and take classes for photography and painting. It was hard to get into some of the classes because they filled up quickly. When no spots were left, some people got angry and tried to start fights.

Ba, Ma, Du, and Tam took turns trying to enter a class so they could share with the rest of the family what they learned. But the only one able to get into a class was Du. Every other day for an hour, he learned about some of the holidays that Americans celebrated. When he got back to his family, he tried to tell them everything he remembered.

"There was a holiday about love, some kind of valley day. A day about a leprechaun and a bunny," said Du.

"A bunny?" asked Ma.

"What's a lepre?" asked Quynh.

"A leprechaun," said Du. "A little man with a pot of gold at the end of the rainbow."

Quynh and Nhu laughed.

By the time January arrived, there was still no word yet from the sponsorship on if and when they would leave for America. They had all the paperwork turned in, and officials had said it would take only a couple of months.

They had already waited six months.

Ba and Du got on another ferry to Hong Kong to find out what went wrong. They headed for the U.S. Consulate General building. It towered fifty stories above them. The American flag was hanging above the doors, slowly waving in the wind.

Before Ba entered, he tightened his grip on the paperwork. Du put a hand on his brother's shoulder. "You got this, brother. I'll wait out here for you."

Ba shared a smile with his brother, took a deep breath, and entered the building.

Inside was a desk, behind which was a security guard. The walls, painted eggshell white, were adorned with framed photos of the Statue of Liberty, Mount Rushmore, and the Golden Gate Bridge.

The guard stood when he saw Ba enter. "Hello. How can I help you all this evening?" he asked.

"I want to see an American. I have paperwork," said Ba.

"I'm sorry, but I can't let you just enter through. Do you have an appointment?"

Behind the guard was another office, where an African American was filing some paperwork. Ba ran past the guard and opened the office doors.

"Hey!" shouted the guard.

The man closed a file cabinet and saw Ba holding some paperwork, with the guard right behind him.

"Please, I have paperwork," said Ba.

The guard entered the room. "I'm so sorry, Mr.—"

The man held up his hand. "It's all right, Frank. I'll help this gentleman."

The guard nodded and left, closing the door behind him. The office was small and comfortable. There was a window that looked out at a little garden. One wall, painted a light blue, had a painting of the American flag. Standing on the desk were two framed photos: one of the man and his wife, the other of three boys.

The man cleared his throat and gestured for Ba to take a seat. "How may I help you?" he asked, sitting in his chair across from Ba.

"I'm a refugee. Filled out paperwork to go to America. They told me it would take only a couple of months, but it's almost been six. I was an officer in the military, fought in the Vietnam War with the Americans," said Ba. He held out the paperwork, which the man took. "My in-laws live in America. This is the copy of the paperwork."

"OK, Mr. ...?"

"Nguyen," said Ba.

"All right, Mr. Nguyen. Let me go and see what happened in the process. I won't be long," said the man. He stood and left the office.

After ten minutes, the man returned. "Thank you for your patience, Mr. Nguyen," the man said. He sat down, holding his tie against his torso. "I want to apologize on behalf of the embassy. It looks like your paperwork was lost. What you handed me—your case—should have already been closed. You and your family should be in America already." The man handed a copy of the paperwork to Ba. "I promise you, I'll personally do your case and fill out all the required paperwork. You'll be my top priority. I'll get you and your family to America in February."

Ba stood and bowed his head. "Thank you, thank you so much Mr. ...?"

The man held out his hand. "Lewis."

Ba glanced at the man's hand and shook it. "Thank you, Mr. Lewis."

"Of course, Mr. Nguyen."

Going to America

February 2, 1980

Three days after Ba's meeting, back at camp, a man stopped by the bulletin board and stabbed a piece of paper onto it with a pushpin.

News was posted there daily about events and about who was going to what country. People checked it daily for the announcement of when they were going to head out to their new country.

Ba, holding his cigarette, waited his turn in line. When he got to the front, he lifted his finger and went down the list of names.

Nga and Phu Nguyen and Family

Ba smiled. They were approved at last. He and his family were required to do a final health check, get fingerprinted, and have X-rays done. A date was listed for when a van would come to pick them up.

A van came the next day to take them to a hospital. They were poked, prodded, and had X-rays taken.

They had to wait a couple of days to get their results back, and once they did, they passed with flying colors. No one was sick or had any diseases.

One day shortly after learning about their final approval for resettlement, Ba and Ma walked toward the bulletin board and passed a pile of bodies covered with blankets. Trucks would tow in boats that were filled with dead people. The bodies were carried off the boats, laid on the ground, and covered with blankets.

Ba wrapped his arm around Ma and walked faster. They weren't able to see the bodies anymore, but they couldn't get away from the cries of family members sitting or standing next to their deceased loved ones.

Two weeks later, a man came to the bulletin board and stuck pieces of paper onto it. Ba and Ma went to it together this time.

Nga Nguyen - 7 people

They were to leave for America in one week. Ma put a hand over her mouth and began to cry. Ba hugged her tight against him, tears in his eyes.

"We're going home," cried Ma.

Ba kissed her head and rocked her against him. "We did it."

Ma pulled back and kissed Ba. "No, you did it. You did all of this."

For the last time, Ba went back to downtown Hong Kong and took Ma with him. Both wanted to get new clothes to appear in tip-top shape when they got to America. Bà Ngoại sent five hundred dollars for the last time.

Ma bought dresses for the girls and Tam, and Ba bought an Omega watch.

They packed their suitcases. Ba and Ma went up to other families and gave them their cooking supplies. The families thanked them and bowed their heads deeply.

Back at their sleeping quarters, Ba picked up Nhu and turned to Ma. "Let's go outside and celebrate."

Ma picked up Dai Duong, and Du grabbed Quynh's hand. All went outside and walked around the camp. They heard clapping and music in the distance.

"Do we all feel like listening to some music?" asked Ba.

"Yeah!" the girls shouted.

Ma nodded in agreement, and all seven of them headed to the music.

There was a stage with three people playing instruments. One had a *dan ty ba*, a traditional Vietnamese string instrument similar to a guitar; the person in the middle had a bamboo flute; and the third had a *t'rung*, a bamboo xylophone. People were gathered around the stage, clapping and dancing.

Ba took his daughters to the group and started dancing with them. Nhu and Quynh giggled. They both were twirled, their dark hair spinning along with them.

Ma hung out near the back, slightly rocking Dai Duong. Tam and Du had joined the dancing.

Ba thought back to the years of 1968 to 1972, when he was the lead singer of a rock 'n' roll cover band consisting of his close friends. There were five people in the band. They covered Beatles songs, Elvis Presley songs, and popular Vietnamese songs. They were invited to play at concerts performed on fields and in concert halls. They were even invited to play on TV shows.

Ma and Tam encouraged Ba to jump on stage and sing. He did so and performed a song. The people in the crowd clapped their hands to the beat.

Ma looked up at her husband and smiled, remembering when he used to play in the band. In a popular concert hall, the stage would be in the spotlight, the crowd in darkness. Ba would pour his heart and soul into the microphone, his friends playing their instruments behind him. People in the audience would cheer, clap their hands, sing along, and dance to the music. Ma would dress her best with a little makeup and go with her friends. They always told her how lucky she was—and, boy, were they right.

After enjoying the music and dancing, the family went back to their building. Ba settled the girls in the top bunk.

"Guess what, girls?" he said.

"What?" asked Quynh.

"We're going to America," said Ba.

Nhu and Quynh smiled.

"Really?" asked Quynh.

"Yes, we'll be out of Hong Kong soon and on our way to America on an airplane."

"We're going to fly?" asked Nhu.

Ba smiled and kissed his daughters on the foreheads. "Yeah, we're going to fly."

Home at Last

February 13, 1980

A van picked them up early the next morning. Ba and his family were nervous and excited to finally leave the refugee camps and be on their way to America.

They were to leave Hong Kong on February 13, 1980, on a Pan Am flight. Their scheduled departure time was eight o'clock in the morning. Awaiting them was a long journey. They had stops in Tokyo, Los Angeles, and Denver before finally arriving in Springfield, where Ma's family was eagerly awaiting them.

Getting caught up in the excitement, Ba and the others put on their best clothes to impress. Ma and Tam wore traditional Vietnamese dresses called áo *dài*. These dresses were worn by women, and sometimes men, on special occasions. Nhu and Quynh wore beautifully pressed dresses in pastel pink and lilac. Ba wore a black-and-white suit, while Du wore slacks and a dress shirt.

On the plane, they put their two small suitcases in the overhead compartment. Ba sat between Nhu and Quynh. Tam and Ma, who was holding Dai Duong, sat together. Du was able to get a window seat right behind Ba and the girls. Quynh looked out the airplane window and watched men in bright vests put suitcases and luggage on a conveyor belt. She watched small bright-pink bags and giant black ones disappear below as if the plane had a mouth and was eating each one.

They waited patiently until all passengers were on the plane. A woman went to the front of the aisle and began to demonstrate how to put on a seatbelt. Ba helped Quynh and Nhu with their seatbelts. Nhu somehow got hers into a knot. The woman in the front then pointed out the exit signs and lights. She pointed to a mask that fell out from above, and she showed the passengers how to put it on. She next demonstrated, in case of a water landing, how to put on the life vest that was located under each seat. Also, passengers could use their seat as a floatation device.

Ba was very fascinated with these airplanes. He hadn't expected them to be this safe, secure, and big.

Next, the flight attendants showed a safety-information card located in the seat-back pocket in front of everyone. Ba took it out and glanced at it, reading it to the best of his ability.

The engine roared to life, and Nhu and Quynh put their arms around their father. He chuckled and kissed the tops of their heads. "It's going to be OK," he said.

The girls buried their heads in Ba's arms. The airplane went backward, drove forward, and paused. Quynh glanced out the window, and all of a sudden, the engine roared again and the plane raced forward. Her body slammed against her seat. She buried her head in her dad's arm. The plane lifted into the sky, and they rose high. Quynh and Nhu didn't dare move until the plane was still. Ba took a deep breath and saw his girls peeking around.

"See? That wasn't so bad," he said with his heart beating fast.

The seatbelt sign was turned off. Soon, Ba smelled smoke in the air and widened his eyes as he saw people smoking. Flight attendants handed out blankets and pillows. Everyone was given something to drink—water for the children and alcohol for the parents. Next, the flight attendants handed out full meals on warm plates.

The food served was tolerable. The bread roll was soggy, slices of ham tasted like rubber, the mashed potatoes had chunks in it, and the carrots were rock hard. They ate it nonetheless, putting something in their bellies.

When the first leg of their flight was almost complete, the seatbelt signs were turned on and the plane descended into Tokyo.

The girls put their hands over their ears as they began to pop.

When the plane landed, everyone unlatched their seatbelts, retrieved their carry-ons, and walked off the plane.

At the gate, Quynh tugged at Ba's arm. "Ba, my ears hurt."

"Me too," whined Nhu.

"I hear gum helps. Let's go get some."

Once the girls started chewing gum and were able to ease the pain in their ears, Ba picked up their checked luggage. "All right. Let's head to our gate to head to Los Angeles."

"We have to get on another plane?" asked Quynh.

Nhu stroked her ears. "I don't want to fly."

Tam grabbed the girls' hands and followed Ba. "You girls don't want to fly anymore? How many people did you know who could fly?"

Quynh and Nhu shook their heads. "None."

"Well, guess what? You girls can fly, fly like birds, and have been high up into the sky with the clouds. How many people can do that?"

They arrived in snowy Denver at three o'clock in the afternoon the same day. They had three hours to spare until their final trip to Springfield.

Quynh looked around with wide, curious eyes. Never in her life had she seen so many people with different colors of hair and eyes. Also, everyone appeared so tall. She felt as small as a mouse compared with those giraffes.

The U.S. Catholic Conference was helping refugees settle in America. Nuns and other volunteers waited for refugees at various airports and assisted them with any questions. They did this on behalf of the U.S. government.

Nuns were the first people to walk up to Ba and his family and welcome them. "Excuse me," said one. "Your flight to Missouri has been canceled. The weather conditions are worse there, and it's unsafe to fly right now."

Another nun walked next to her. "We'll take you to a hotel."

A hotel shuttle came and got them—and the nuns accompanied them. The family tried to bury themselves in their coats, trying to cover as much of their skin against the snow as they could. The girls were mesmerized and tried to catch snowflakes in their hands or on the tips of their tongues. By the time they entered the hotel lobby, everyone was shivering, not being used to such frigid weather.

While the nuns went to the check-in desk, Nhu tugged on Ba's sleeve. "Ba, I'm hungry and thirsty."

Another nun walked to them. "Just around a corner is a vending machine. In the meantime, here's a ten-dollar voucher for the restaurant upstairs."

The nun handed a slip of paper to Ba.

For the remainder of their stay in Denver, they mostly waited in their hotel rooms. Ba, Ma, and the kids were in one room, Tam and Du were in another room. They counted down the hours until they could return to the airport, fly on a plane, and finally be reunited with their family in Missouri.

To pass the time, they flipped through the channels on the TV, laughing at the commercials and the way the people on the screen spoke English. They also toured the hotel, watching people swim in the pool, wear their best clothes, and carry around suitcases.

They made it to Missouri the next day.

As the plane was about to land, Nhu pressed her face against the window. Ma gently pried her away from it.

"Where's Bà Ngoại and Ông Ngoại?" asked Nhu, anxious to see her grandparents.

Ma looked out the window and smiled. "They're at the airport waiting for us."

Outside, there was a thick white blanket covering everything. The houses looked like gingerbread, and the trees looked like giant snowflakes.

The plane landed, and Ma felt her heart flutter. Her chest felt as light as a helium-filled balloon. It had been too long—so many years—since she last saw her family. She hadn't been sure whether this moment would even happen since that heart-wrenching farewell on the docks back in Vietnam nearly five years before.

As they got off the plane, Ma looked down at Dai Duong and smiled. Her mother would get to meet her newest granddaughter.

When they got off the plane, Ba squeezed Ma's hand. "You feeling OK?"

Ma gave him half a smile. "I'm so nervous. Why am I nervous?"

Ba chuckled and rubbed Ma's back as they exited the building. Everyone shivered in the cold. Ma looked around and saw familiar faces next to the curb. Ba took Dai Duong from Ma as she ran to her family.

Bà Ngoại saw her oldest daughter, and tears came streaming down her face. Bà Ngoại met Ma halfway and hugged her tight. "You made it. By God, thank you. You made it."

Ma held her mom very close, burying her face in her coat. Ma breathed in her scent, and memories from her childhood came back.

Bà Ngoại pulled back, brushed Ma's hair from her face, and kissed her tears. "I'm finally at peace. Our families are back together."

Ba and the girls stepped forward. Bà Ngoại hugged her granddaughters tight, and Ba held out Dai Duong. Bà Ngoại put a hand to her mouth as more tears came to her eyes. She held her youngest grandchild. Dai Duong cooed, and Bà Ngoại kissed her forehead.

"Hello, Dai Duong. I'm your Bà ngoại." Bà Ngoại looked up at Ma and snuggled Dai Duong against her. "She's beautiful."

Ba put his arm around Ma. "She was our miracle."

Bà Ngoại and everyone gathered in a group hug. Ông Ngoại was the first to step back. "Let's take you home."

Ba, smiling as tears came to his eyes, still couldn't believe they were standing on American soil.

He thought about what he had endured, from the battlefields where he had been wounded twice by enemy fire, to the hunger and brutality at the reeducation camps.

They put their bags in the car and got in. Ba looked back at the airport and thought about what it had taken to get there: sailing across the surging ocean, Ma giving birth in the middle of the night on the boat, getting stranded at sea, getting stuck on an island, making it to Hong Kong, moving from camp to camp, waiting to be approved, and being checked all the time on their health and background.

Ba looked at his family as Bà Ngoại asked them how their flight was. He looked at his daughters' smiles, his wife's relaxed posture, and his siblings' hopeful eyes. Back in Vietnam, none were safe and none felt welcome anymore. Ever since they had arrived in the United States, Americans had treated them with kindness. All felt welcome, comfortable, and safe.

Through the car window, Ba looked at every house they passed and envisioned his family there. They had finally made it—they were in the land of opportunity, the land of the free, and the land of dreams.

They had finally made it to a place they could call home.

Epilogue

Where Are They Now?

Ba and Ma (Phu and Nga)
Moved from Springfield, settled in Denver in the 1980s, and have lived there ever since. They raised their family of five kids—three girls and two boys (Quynh, Nhu, Duong, HT, and Denver). Both Phu and Nga are retired after working their entire adult lives in various manufacturing jobs. Nga worked for several companies including AT&T for eleven years. Phu worked as a technician for a data-storage company for more than twenty years.

Quynh
Graduated from the University of Colorado Boulder with a degree in journalism. She spent nearly fifteen years reporting the news at TV stations in Rochester, Minnesota; Norfolk, Virginia; and Denver, Colorado. She earned three Emmy Awards for her work in the TV industry. She resides in Colorado with her husband and two kids.

Nhu
Graduated from the University of Colorado Boulder with a double major in computer information systems and finance. She resides in Colorado with her husband and three boys.

Dai Duong
Graduated from the University of Colorado Boulder with a finance degree and got her Master of Business Administration degree from Regis University. She resides in Colorado with her husband and two kids.

HT
Attended Metropolitan State University of Denver. He currently lives in California.

Denver
Graduated from the University of Colorado Boulder with a finance degree and got his Master of Business Administration degree from the University of Texas at Austin. He currently resides in Colorado.

Tam
Currently lives in California with her husband. They have two daughters. Tam retired from the U.S. Postal Service after working there for more than twenty-five years.

Du
Currently lives in California with his wife. They have two children. Du and his wife have a successful Vietnamese restaurant.

Ba's Family
Bà Nội and Ông Nội made it out of Vietnam in 1991 and resettled in the United States after Ba worked to sponsor them there. The rest of his

siblings relocated to the United States in 1998 and 1999. Bà Nội passed away in 2018 at the age of ninety-five. Ông Nội passed away in 2010 at the age of ninety-three.

Ma's Family
Bà Ngoại relocated from Missouri to California in 1996. She currently lives there with one of her daughters. She is ninety-five years old. Ông Ngoại passed away in 1985 at the age of fifty-six.

Son
Relocated with his family to Toronto.

BBC Crew
The documentary on "boat people" did air on TV. The news crew sent a VHS copy to Ma's parents in Missouri. The family loaned it to a friend and the tape was lost. Ba and Ma still have the photographs taken by the news crew.

Acknowledgements

Writing this book was challenging and exhilarating. It is a dream come true to have a legacy to pass on to my family. I want to thank the people who helped make it happen.

To my parents, Ba and Ma. You are the inspiration for this project. Thank you for your courage and bravery. I am forever indebted to you both.

To my husband, Matt. You stood by me during my struggles as well as my successes. Thank you for your love and encouragement. I am eternally grateful to you.

To my children, Madison and Joshua. All my love to both of you. May you always remember your roots.

To my siblings, Nhu, Duong, HT, and Denver. My heartfelt thanks for motivating me to get this book done. May we never forget the sacrifices our parents made so we could have this beautiful life.

To Jordyn Martinez. Thank you for your hard work and valuable contributions. You are an amazing young talent. I truly appreciate everything you did to help me during this journey.

To my copyeditor, Dale Ulland. My sincere gratitude for your advice, suggestions, and keen insight. You made this book better.

To my copyeditor, Kristy Phillips. Your knowledge of Vietnamese history was a tremendous asset. Thank you for your guidance during this process.

About the Author

Quynh Nguyen Forss was five years old when her family fled Vietnam in search of a better life. They resettled in Colorado, where she grew up. Quynh has a bachelor's degree in journalism from the University of Colorado Boulder. She went on to work at television stations across the country for nearly fifteen years as a reporter and producer. She earned three Emmy Awards for her work in the industry. Quynh lives in Colorado with her husband, Matt. They have two children, Madison and Joshua.

www.ingramcontent.com/pod-product-compliance
Lightning Source LLC
Chambersburg PA
CBHW070709130626
46553CB00005B/1905